A New Concept of
Cooperative Security

Brookings Occasional Papers

A New Concept of Cooperative Security

ASHTON B. CARTER
WILLIAM J. PERRY
JOHN D. STEINBRUNER

THE BROOKINGS INSTITUTION

Washington, D.C.

Brookings Occasional Papers

THE BROOKINGS INSTITUTION is a private nonprofit organization devoted to research, education, and publication on important issues of domestic and foreign policy. Its principal purpose is to bring knowledge to bear on the major policy problems facing the American people.

On occasion Brookings staff members produce research papers that warrant immediate circulation as contributions to the public debate on current issues of national importance. Because of the speed of their production, these Occasional Papers are not subjected to all of the formal review procedures established for the Institution's research publications, and they may be revised at a later date. As in all Brookings publications, the judgments, conclusions, and recommendations presented in the Papers are solely those of the authors and should not be attributed to the trustees, officers, or other staff members of the Institution.

Copyright © 1992 by
THE BROOKINGS INSTITUTION
1775 Massachusetts Avenue, N.W., Washington, D.C.

ISBN 0-8157-8145-8

Library of Congress Catalog Number 92-074426

9 8 7 6 5 4 3 2 1

Acknowledgements

This paper is the initial product of a research project examining how principles of cooperative security might be applied to problems of controlling weapons proliferation. The project was initiated and is being financially supported by the Carnegie Corporation of New York. It was jointly organized by the Brookings Institution, the Carnegie Endowment for International Peace, Harvard University, and Stanford University. In addition to the three authors of this paper the project steering committee includes Geoffrey Kemp, Janne Nolan, and Leonard Spector. A collaborative volume presenting the overall results of the project and other supporting publications are also being prepared.

The three authors are personally responsible for the contents of the paper, but it has been developed through an extensive dialogue with other participants in the project. Four major workshops and a full conference have been held to discuss the topics addressed in this paper. The participants in these sessions have had substantial influence on the paper, some of them by means of their cogent and spirited disagreements. The authors therefore wish to acknowledge the contributions of the following people with special gratitude, while exonerating them from any direct responsibility for what it contains:

Kanti Bajpai, David Bernstein, Coit Blacker, George Bunn, Abram Chayes, Antonia Handler Chayes, Stephen Cohen, Owen Cote, Jonathan Dean, Francis Deng, Kenneth Flamm, Alexander George, Mikhail Gerasev, Harry Harding, John Harvey, Catherine Kelleher, Geoffrey Kemp, Andrei Kokoshin, Michael Krepon, John Lewis, Michael May, Steven E. Miller, Janne Nolan, William Potter, Wolfgang Reinicke, Alexander Rondos, Yahya Sadowski, James Schear, Leonard Spector, Paul Stares, Mitchel Wallerstein, and Charles Zraket.

Adrianne Goins and Michael Levin provided research assistance for this paper. Micahel Barre, Susan Blanchard, Charlotte Brady, Brian Davenport, Rosemary Hamerton-Kelly, Laura Holgate, Barbara Heymann, and Susanne Lane gave administrative support. Theresa Walker and Patricia Dewey edited the manuscript; Susan F. Woollen typeset the paper. Their support is also gratefully acknowledged.

On behalf of all the project participants the authors wish to thank the Carnegie Corporation of New York, the W. Alton Jones Foundation, Inc., and the John D. and Catherine T. MacArthur Foundation for their financial support.

THE ENDING OF THE COLD WAR and the dissolution of the Soviet Union have transformed the driving problems of international security. The fear of massive aggression in Europe can no longer serve as the central focus for defense planning among the leading nations. The dissolution of the Warsaw Pact and finally of the Soviet Union have definitively dispelled that traditional preoccupation. The problem of countering armed aggression has been replaced in nations of both East and West with pressing defense planning problems of an entirely different character. The enormous existing military establishments labor under two great burdens: coping with the problems posed by surplus weapons, soldiers, and military industries as a dramatic demobilization from the force levels of the cold war proceeds; and restructuring themselves in size and composition without the benefit of well-defined missions or "threats." Meanwhile new nations created out of the former USSR struggle to conceptualize their place in the security order and their resulting defense requirements. They look to the rest of the international community to indicate how they should relate to emerging new security structures and norms.

Similarly, the once riveting fear that nuclear weapons might be used deliberately—in a global war, or to support political intimidation, or in a calculated surprise attack—has receded in significance. Already in the closing years of the cold war it had begun to be acknowledged that virtually all plausible varieties of deterrence of such deliberate attack could be underwritten with a fraction of the existing nuclear arsenals. In the wake of the cold war this proposition seems unlikely to be contested politically.

With core deterrence so securely established, the safe management of nuclear weapons has become a greater priority than refining the principles of deterrent stability. Once again, security issues of a new and different order present themselves. Uncoiling the readiness posture of strategic arsenals so that they present less risk of inadvertent use is an unfinished task that will require some policy push to accomplish, in view of the ingrained habits of military organizations and command and control systems. Meanwhile, a problem of deep historic significance is

1

unfolding as the destiny of the nuclear arsenal of the former USSR is debated among the successor states, and as these states face a very real prospect of further disintegration and chaos into which the nuclear arsenal could be swept. Finally, the conduct of potential new nuclear proliferators around the world will be influenced in some measure by the example set by established nuclear powers. The success of the heirs of the cold war in safely managing and reducing their arsenals and in relegating nuclear weapons to a background role in security affairs can have a powerful effect on their ability to stem nuclear proliferation in other regions of the world. Together, these new challenges amount to a transformed agenda for nuclear weapons policy.

These changes alter the formative conditions of security policy. At the beginning of the cold war, the United States established two principal new security objectives: containment of conventional aggression along the periphery of the Soviet Union and deterrence of nuclear attack by threat of massive retaliation. In support of these objectives, the United States initiated a major rearmament program with primary emphasis on nuclear weapons and formed a number of collective security regimes, most notably NATO. Over the course of forty years the implementation of these policies created a large military establishment continuously prepared for war on short notice—a few minutes in the case of nuclear weapons and a few weeks in the case of conventional weapons. From 1950 through 1992 the United States spent $11.5 trillion in 1992 dollars to create and maintain this security posture—an average of more than 7.5 percent of its total economic product for the period. The political, institutional, conceptual, and emotional commitments supporting this investment were correspondingly strong, providing a primary organizing purpose for the entire U.S. political system.

In the course of this effort, the United States developed several consensus judgments about its relative strengths and vulnerabilities and derived from these evaluations the central elements of its security doctrine. During the 1950s and 1960s, the strategic nuclear forces of the United States were considered superior to those of the Soviet Union, while the reverse was believed true of conventional forces. The chief security treaties, North Atlantic Treaty Organization (NATO), Southeast Asia Treaty Organization (SEATO), and Central Treaty Organization (CENTO), were formed on that premise and on the belief that matching the conventional force assets of the Soviet alliance system would be unacceptably costly. Allied conventional forces, particularly those of NATO, were explicitly deployed as a credible trigger for the use of U.S. nuclear forces in the event of a conventional attack not affecting the United States itself.

During the 1970s and 1980s, however, Soviet nuclear weapons deployments achieved what was considered effective parity, and alliance doctrines were adjusted to that new assessment. NATO decided to improve the capability of its conventional forces but still did not consider it economically feasible to match the size of the opposing alliance forces, particularly those in forward deployment. NATO therefore embarked on a program to counter the numerical superiority of opposing forces with qualitative improvements in its own weapons, increased spending on conventional defenses, and increased cooperation among its member nations. This strategy, called the "offset strategy," was pursued by most of the European NATO nations and by five successive American administrations during the 1970s and 1980s. Since this strategy was based on the technological superiority of the West, a corollary part of the strategy sought to strengthen controls on the transfer of Western technology to countries in the Soviet bloc. Since the 1950s these controls have been administered by an organization known as the Coordinating Committee for Multilateral Export Controls (or COCOM), whose members consisted of all NATO nations except Iceland, plus Japan and Australia.

After two decades of development and production, the United States has realized some of the fruits of the "offset strategy." In particular, it has deployed the first elements of the new configuration of conventional military power, which Russian writers term the "reconnaissance strike complex." The U.S. reconnaissance strike complex demonstrated overwhelming effectiveness in the Gulf War's Desert Storm when used against an army with conventional armored forces and conventional air defense systems. The initial success of this technology, which was in fact well short of its full potential in the Desert Storm operation, suggests that the problem of conventional defense—the major perceived deficiency throughout the cold war—was effectively solved just as it disappeared. To add to this irony the solution brings forth entirely new forms of military capability destined to present entirely new security problems. The same assets that can prevent ground armies from seizing territory can wreak precisely designed havoc on any organized activity from long range. That is a form of intrusiveness never before experienced.

This sequence of developments has important consequences even for nations that were not direct participants in either the cold war or the Gulf War. The animosities that fuel regional conflict are usually long-standing and local. Yet they are influenced by the prevailing world security order. During the cold war, this influence took the form of client relationships between regional powers and the contending superpower blocs. With the superpower standoff now thawed, regional conflicts are less likely to lead to global war, but also less likely to be forestalled or moderated by the protagonists' patrons. In the wake of the Gulf War some regional powers are concerned about potential domination by a great power coalition. Others may be inclined to pursue traditional antagonisms with modern methods. With ready access to weapons technology and enlarged political scope, the independent security judgments of regional powers will significantly affect the evolution of international security conditions.

Together, these transformations have greatly reduced the immediate danger of large-scale military conflict but have also created some demanding new problems of managing international security in the longer term. This shift poses a conceptual crisis for security establishments around the world. There is a corresponding need for new principles to ensure that the pending reconfiguration of these military establishments is steered toward safe and stable outcomes.

For U.S. security policy in particular, the conceptual crisis is acute. The USSR is gone; Iraq's military machine is defeated. The absence of immediate threat is welcome, but also disorienting. Countering threats and deterring through readiness are the traditional bases for defense planning. Yet in both conventional and nuclear realms, today's defense policy problems are not anchored in immediate threat.

The absence of well-defined threat cannot be equated with the absence of danger to U.S. security, however. The unfolding dramas in Eastern Europe and the former Soviet Union, and regional animosities around the world, pose a serious danger of conflict that would be harmful to U.S. interests, directly and indirectly. Proliferation of destructive technology casts a shadow over future U.S. security in a way that cannot be directly addressed through superior force or readiness. Serious economic and environmental problems point to an inescapable interdependence of U.S. interests with the interests of other nations. And even when U.S. interests are not directly at risk, the United States bears an unavoidable responsibility for the world order.

In response to the transformation of the strategic landscape, a restructuring of the U.S. defense posture is under way. The adjustments are extensive, affecting nuclear and conventional forces, organizational roles and missions, and the defense industry. Some of this restructuring is required by arms control agreements, but much of it is a nearly spontaneous reaction to budget reductions that are themselves the political consequence of a lessened perception of threat. Most attempts to guide this restructuring have consisted of redefinitions of threat: a reconstituted superpower Russia, for nuclear forces; one or several implicit replays of the Gulf War, for conventional forces. That U.S. security policy might instead be primarily directed to preventing such threats from arising is an idea that has not yet taken hold. The desirable size of U.S. conventional and nuclear forces, the appropriate rate of modernization, and the degree of combat readiness to be maintained have not been assessed from this perspective.

In the aftermath of the Persian Gulf War, the United States is generally conceded to possess a power projection capability, based on the reconnaissance strike complex, that no other military establishment can match, not without also matching the lengthy and intense investment that created it. For more than a decade to come, therefore, no other military establishment will be able to contemplate any major offensive without acknowledging that the United States is capable of decisive countermeasures. That inevitably makes the United States, in the estimation of most countries, the ultimate answer to acts of aggression; for some it also makes the United States a potential problem.

But comfort in U.S. superiority in conventional military capability is tempered by the realization that it is heavily circumscribed, and quite possibly temporary. Most countries will be reasonably confident that as a matter of practical politics the United States would not initiate any significant military action without some form of broad international approval. That is, there is an awareness that the superior U.S. conventional military power cannot be used except within some internationally shared framework. That framework awaits definition, however, and protracted delay in providing it would invite suspicion.

Over the longer term, the global diffusion of advanced technology precludes an enduring U.S. military superiority unless that superiority is accepted as serving the general international interest. Superior U.S. conventional power projection is derived primarily from the application of dramatic advances in the collection, processing, and transmission of information. The core technologies that support these decisive military functions are being developed in commercial markets, and access to them cannot be denied. Nor can access be denied to the knowledge and materials required to make weapons of mass destruction, which, because of their destructiveness and the fear they engender, could be seen by an aggressor as a means of offsetting U.S. conventional military power.

As a matter of logic, these radical transformations in the nature of the threat compel commensurately radical revisions in U.S. security policies. The new threats cannot be met solely with readiness and deterrence. The new security problems require more constructive and more sophisticated forms of influence that concentrate more on the initial preparation of military forces than on the final decisions to use them. The pattern of military preparation and investment in other nations is therefore of more consequence for U.S. security than an immediate posture of "threat."

The appropriate principle for dealing with these new security problems is that of cooperative engagement—in essence a commitment to regulate the size, technical composition, investment patterns, and operational practices of all military forces by mutual consent for mutual benefit. The resulting cooperative form of security offers the best prospect of addressing the new problems of the post–cold war world. Thus the development of a regime for cooperative engagement is the new strategic imperative.

In the world of practical politics, however, even the most powerful imperatives are not recognized immediately or fully if they involve sharp departures from the past. Redirecting the thoughts and emotions of large numbers of people usually requires substantial time and often a crystallizing crisis. Fundamental changes in security policy can occur only if a new consensus is formed.

At the moment, the revision of security policy and the formation of a new consensus to support it are still at an early stage. The idea of comprehensive security cooperation among the major military establishments to form an inclusive international security arrangement has been only barely acknowledged and is only partially developed. The basic principle of cooperation has been proclaimed in general terms in the Paris Charter issued by Conference on Security and Cooperation in Europe (CSCE) members in November of 1990. Important implementing provisions have been embodied in the Strategic Arms Reductions Talks (START), Conventional Forces in Europe (CFE), and Intermediate-Range Nuclear

Forces (INF) treaties. Except for the regulation of U.S. and Common-wealth of Independent States (CIS) strategic forces, however, these arrangements apply only to the European theater and even there have not been systematically developed. The formation of a new security order requires that cooperative security arrangements be extended to other forces and potential theaters of military engagement. Clearly that exercise will stretch the minds of all those whose thinking about security has been premised on confrontational methods.

Nonetheless, such a stretching is unavoidable. The new security problems are driven by powerful forces reshaping the entire international context. They impose starkly different requirements. They will deflect even the impressive momentum of U.S. military traditions. The eventual outcome is uncertain. It turns upon political debates yet to be held, consensus judgments yet to form, and events and their implications yet to unfold. Fundamental reconceptualization of security policy is a necessary step in the right direction, and it is important to get on with it. Getting on with it means defining the new concept of cooperative security, identifying the trends that motivate it, outlining its implications for practical policy action, and acknowledging its constraints. These tasks are the purpose of this essay.

The Concept of Cooperative Security

The central purpose of cooperative security arrangements is to prevent war and to do so primarily by preventing the means for successful aggression from being assembled, thus also obviating the need for states so threatened to make their own counterpreparations. Cooperative security thus displaces the centerpiece of security planning from preparing to counter threats to preventing such threats from arising—from deterring aggression to making preparation for it more difficult. In the process, the potential destructiveness of military conflict—especially the use of weapons of mass destruction—is also reduced. Cooperative security differs from the traditional idea of collective security as preventive medicine differs from acute care. Cooperative security is designed to ensure that organized aggression cannot start on any large scale. Collective security, however, is an arrangement for deterring aggression through counterthreat and defeating it if it occurs.

Clearly the one idea does not preclude the other and both are, in fact, mutually reinforcing. A fully developed cooperative security framework would include provisions for collective security as a residual guarantee to its members. Systematic prevention of dangerous or aggressive military postures would make these residual guarantees easier to convey because they would be less likely to be required and, in the event, easier to underwrite. The cooperative security idea assumes that war is not inevitable, as disease and death are, and that commitment to prevention can aspire to be indefinitely effective.

To meet this aspiration, it is presumed that cooperation would ideally be comprehensive, including all important features of military capability as well as all major military establishments. The arrangement would restrain the ground forces and tactical air assets that provide the firepower for offensive operations. It would less stringently limit systems that are more or less unambiguously defensive and that can only be used to resist offensive intrusion on national territory. It would restrict nuclear weapons deployments to background deterrent functions only, ensure high standards of safety for the security and control of these weapons, and constrain further innovation and deployment of nuclear weapons to existing types and to existing nuclear weapons states. It would eliminate all other weapons of mass destruction. It would provide transparency so that all military establishments are informed of the military preparations of others and significant violations of the arrangement cannot be concealed. It would have enforceable sanctions and positive incentives to induce compliance and to halt attempted violations. The resulting limits on equipping and operating military forces would be consensual and universally shared.

Since they are to be established by consent rather than imposed by threat of force, cooperative security arrangements must be based on premises that can be widely accepted as legitimate. Such arrangements should also be inclusive in the sense that all countries are eligible to belong to them as long as they conform to its rules. Indeed the spirit of cooperative security is to ensure that all countries do belong and do conform. This requires incentives to induce voluntary compliance and also careful construction of the rules to be sure they can be reasonably judged to be equitable from a universal perspective.

Such a cooperative security order need not take the form of a single, all-encompassing legal regime or arms control agreement, but would probably begin with a set of overlapping, mutually reinforcing arrangements derived from agreements already in force. In fact, a look at the rich fabric of constraints that have grown up in more or less unconnected fashion indicates that ingredients of cooperative security are not hard to find on the international landscape. These range from limits on military operations, such as various confidence- and security-building measures (CSBMs) in Europe and the Middle East and agreements covering accidents, hotlines, and crisis centers between the superpowers, to limits on force size and weapons types—for example, START, CFE, and INF agreements and the nuclear, biological, and chemical weapons nonproliferation regimes. They extend to cooperative verification and transparency measures, such as the data exchanges and on-site inspections required by arms control agreements, the U.N. Permanent Five arms sale registry, and the new Open Skies agreement. They are embodied in formal agreements like START and CFE and in informal regimes like COCOM and the London and Australia groups. And they are embodied in tacit but firmly established norms of international behavior, such as those condemning use of weapons of mass destruction or changing of borders by force.

Military establishments around the world already are entangled in a large web of internationally sanctioned restraints on how they equip themselves and operate in peacetime. Cooperative security means making the effort to thicken and unify this web. Spinning the web must become a more conscious, central objective of international security policy. Many of the existing restraints grew up in the cold war. The end of the cold war is not an occasion to abandon the spinning of this web, but an opportunity to make the web more comprehensive. Though the rules embodied in the web will require adaptation to the peculiar security dilemmas of different regions, all regions should be encompassed by it.

Thus, cooperative security is, and probably will remain, an aspiration that will be only incompletely fulfilled. It is not a description of the world system, a prediction about the future, or a theory of international relations. But aspirations give coherence to security policy. They define what is desirable and partly, if incompletely, achievable. Organizing principles like deterrence, nuclear stability, and containment embodied the aspirations of the cold war, and they were invaluable in guiding thought and action. Cooperative security is the corresponding principle for international security in the post–cold war era.

For the United States, Russia, and the European powers previously locked in military confrontation, cooperative security is the right principle with which to guide their disengagement and the massive demobilization of their military establishments and industries. Cooperative security also offers a new and shared framework for the major powers to influence regional conflict and stem proliferation. For many other states long engaged in regional confrontation, cooperative security provides a new framework for the international community to provide reassurance and stability, replacing the rigid East-West alignments of the past and preempting reliance on a superpower-led collective security that many smaller countries fear and distrust. And for new nations born from the breakup of the USSR, for newly powerful nations like Japan and Germany seeking a security identity, and for emerging regional powers, cooperative security defines a responsible path of self-expression.

It would be easy to gain consensus that an international security arrangement characterized by these various elements of cooperation would be a superior form of international order. With immediate military threats reduced and their development made more controllable, the traditional objectives of deterring war and protecting national territory could be accomplished with substantially smaller forces at a far lower cost. Moreover, direct cooperation would allow more legitimate international influence on the looming restructuring of military establishments in the former blocs of East and West, as well as on the intensifying competition between economic and military investment in the developing world. Prevailing judgment will be highly skeptical, however, on the achievability of such a comprehensive form of cooperative security. It is widely believed, with ample historical support, that sovereign nations cannot be made to conform to cooperative standards.

Like containment and deterrence, therefore, the usefulness of the cooperative security principle depends on establishing its limits. Cooperative security does not aspire to create an international government, to eliminate all weapons, to prevent all forms of violence, to resolve all conflicts, or to harmonize all political values. The focus is on preventing accumulation of the means for serious, deliberate, organized aggression—that is, the seizing of territory by force or the destruction of vital assets by remote bombardment. Focused on restraining the organized preparations of established militaries, cooperative security does not address itself directly to substate violence, which is a principal source of chronic conflict and human misery in the world. But cooperative security provides a framework—indeed, a necessary framework— for the international community to organize responses to civil violence.

Ingredients of a Cooperative Order

An international arrangement incorporating the concept of cooperative security and accepting the consequent constraints must begin with the central principle that the only legitimate purpose of national military forces is the defense of national territory or the participation in multinational forces that enforce U.N. sanctions or maintain peace. That principle is consistent with the declared military doctrines of the major military establishments and is now believed consistent with their real expectations as well. Since it requires that any effort to change borders by force be disavowed, there are political difficulties with it in some parts of the world, particularly in the Middle East. Nonetheless, it is accepted broadly enough and seriously enough to be the most promising foundation for international consensus.

Full adoption of this principle would lead immediately to important conclusions for cooperative design of military forces. National ground forces would be structured for defense of national territory and their territory-taking capabilities would be minimized. National capabilities for deep strike at rear and homeland targets inside the territory of others by missile or long-range aircraft would be constrained. Some of the ground and air forces that are in excess of national requirements could be configured for use in a multinational military force that could enforce U.N. sanctions when necessary. As an egregious form of offensive capability, nuclear weapons would be relegated to a background deterrent role only, and their spread stemmed. Chemical and biological weapons would be banned entirely. Mutual restraint would be verified and reassurances given among cooperating parties through extensive transparency in force deployment and operations and in production, sale, and purchase of weapons.

Background Nuclear Deterrence and Cooperative Denuclearization

The most fertile field for security cooperation is nuclear weapons. Here established traditions of cooperation exist in the form of negotiated superpower arms control and the global nonproliferation regime. Both areas are in need of change, and the direction of change will bring them into greater interrelation and mutual support. The nuclear relationship between the United States and the Soviet Union underwent profound transformation well before the breakup of the Soviet Union, but with its final demise the pace of change has quickened. The reciprocal unilateral pledges of Presidents Bush and Gorbachev in the fall of 1991 led to the withdrawal in a few short months of the forty-year-old deployments of tactical nuclear weapons, which were closely associated with conventional forces and warfighting roles. The START and START follow-on agreements, if ratified and implemented, would mark a similarly bold demobilization of strategic nuclear forces. But nevertheless the need remains to deepen, hasten, and make irreversible the progress that is occurring. To do so requires the inauguration of new forms of security cooperation, new forms of involvement on the part of the international community outside of the United States and former Soviet Union, and realization of new linkages between the cold war nuclear demobilization and the global nonproliferation regime.

Since the dawn of the nuclear age, the threat of global war between East and West beginning in Europe defined the roles and established the salience of nuclear weapons in the defense planning of the major powers. Neither bloc could contemplate defeat in such a contest. Neither would depend on conventional forces alone to prevent such defeat. Thus resort to use of nuclear weapons seemed probable and preparing for use essential. Simple possession of nuclear weapons could not alone slake the thirst for ironclad deterrence in the face of profound distrust of the opponent, and the many possibilities and scenarios for the outbreak of war, given the many theaters of confrontation, seemed to require a commensurate elaboration of nuclear doctrines and forces to cover all conceivable eventualities. The result was large, complex, and diverse nuclear forces marbled amongst the air, naval, and ground forces, a similarly large overlay of intercontinental weapons, and a flowering of theories and plans to apply them.

At hand with the ending of East-West confrontation is the prospect of radical deemphasis of nuclear weapons in the security conceptions of the major powers. In this vision nuclear weapons would stand in the background of the military establishments of the major powers rather than in the foreground. Possession alone would be nine-tenths of deterrence, as it is of the law. Doctrines covering the residual nuclear forces—themselves much shrunken and simplified—would foresee retaliation only, and that only in response to first nuclear use and without any automatic response. Recent pledges by Washington and Moscow to move their forces to "zero alert" and to remove the target instructions from the memories of the guidance computers atop nuclear missiles are metaphors for this transformation of nuclear doctrine. Motivating this transformation is not only a desire to relax the taut and dangerous cold war standoff, but a recognition that nuclear weapons still hold attractions for aspiring lesser powers, even though they no longer serve compelling needs for the great powers. Deemphasizing nuclear weapons in their own security thinking is a necessary, if not sufficient, step by the great powers toward inducing others to deemphasize them.

This transformation takes place in the midst of an ongoing revolution in the former Soviet Union, involving devolution of political authority from the Soviet Union to its fifteen constituent republics and from Moscow and the Communist party to a host of nationalities, factions, and industrial enterprises across Asia. Such political disintegration, and its potential to lead to chaos, is common enough in the world. But this is the first time it has happened in a nuclear nation, and that fact poses unprecedented dangers to nuclear safety.

These dangers are of three sorts. First, the splintering of the Soviet Union could be accompanied by a splintering of its nuclear arsenal. Ukraine and Kazakhstan, for example, would possess the third- and fourth-largest nuclear arsenals in the world—larger than those of Britain, France, and China—if they came into control of the nuclear weapons based on their territory. Second, control of some fraction of the some 30,000 nuclear weapons of the former Soviet Union could be lost through the actions of mutinous military custodians, political factions, opportunists, or terrorists. Third, economic and political chaos could permit the diversion of nuclear materials, expertise, or weapons to parties outside the former Soviet Union, fueling proliferation.

These dangers can only be influenced by the United States and the international community through cooperative engagement with parties in the former Soviet Union. Such dangers do not arise from traditional security dilemmas. Confrontation, deterrence, or adversarial negotiation cannot address them. Avoidance of these dangers depends on the overall economic and political reform and stability of the former Soviet Union, but more specifically on three factors on which the concept of cooperative security bears directly. First, the current political balance in Ukraine and Kazakhstan favors those who agree to the complete, eventual withdrawal of nuclear weapons from the territory of these states and to continued operational control of these weapons from Moscow in the meantime. That acceptance will not endure unless these states remain convinced that their security concerns will be addressed cooperatively by the international community. Second, the military and the managers of the nuclear weapons complex in Russia must remain convinced that the terms of the nuclear demobilization are equitable and, where appropriate, reciprocal. Furthermore they must have their material needs met during and after the demobilization. Third, political leaders in the former Soviet Union must remain focused on the solemn responsibilities of nuclear custodianship despite the press of the economic and political challenges they face, which might understandably tend to divert their attention. Being politicians, they must see a political reward in continuing denuclearization.

Thus the process of staving off the nuclear danger inherent in the ongoing revolution in the former Soviet Union receives important political cover and sustenance from the nuclear deemphasis and demobilization that had begun before the demise of the Soviet Union. Momentum must be maintained. But more direct forms of cooperative engagement are needed.

A significant start at such engagement was stimulated by the U.S. Congress in the Soviet Nuclear Threat Reduction Act of 1991, known as the Nunn-Lugar amendment because its inspiration came from Senators Sam Nunn of Georgia and Richard Lugar of Indiana. This act authorized the executive branch to finance and assist cooperative programs of denuclearization with funds from the Defense Department. The cooperation authorized in the act included (but was not limited to) dismantlement of nuclear and chemical warheads. Defense Department funding signified the security benefits to the United States of keeping denuclearization in the former Soviet Union on track.

Implementation of the Nunn-Lugar amendment was originally lethargic and unimaginative, with bureaucrats on both sides showing difficulty adjusting to the new style of engagement. Nevertheless, eventually plans were laid for assistance in secure storage and transport of nuclear weapons, dismantlement of chemical weapons, research support for weapons scientists and engineers to reorient their efforts to peaceful purposes, and other areas. After some delay the importance of including states of the former Soviet Union other than Russia in the program of cooperation was realized. The Nunn-Lugar amendment succeeded in its principal purpose, which was less to finance specific technical steps than to set an agenda for denuclearization and cooperation, and to command attention to this agenda on the part of political leaders in the former Soviet Union and leaders of the powerful ministries of defense and atomic power of the former Soviet Union, as well as their counterparts in the West.

If denuclearization is to proceed, cooperative engagement in the style of the Nunn-Lugar amendment must be extended and deepened. In this context the inadequacy of traditional negotiated arms control is evident. The framework for a START follow-on agreement, which was agreed to by Presidents Bush and Yeltsin at their Washington summit in June 1992, envisions reductions in strategic arsenals that approach those called for in common notions of "minimal" or "background" deterrence. In this sense the agreement heralds a remarkable deemphasis of nuclear weapons. However, the reductions are not to be completed until 2003.

This decade-long timetable is paced by the elaborate procedures for deactivation of nuclear weapons systems worked out in the original START agreement, which was negotiated with the Soviet Union in the 1980s. Such procedures focus on destruction of launchers rather than on disposition of nuclear warheads or even missiles. Destruction of launchers is to be verifiable and irreversible, and thus its accomplishment takes time. It also costs money, and expense is a frequent reason given by parties in the former Soviet Union who defend the long timetable.

But a decade is several times longer than the probable longevity of at least some of the governments whose cooperation will be necessary to implement the agreement: Russia, Ukraine, Kazakhstan, and Belarus. Delay therefore not only fails to capitalize on the opportunity presented by the end of the cold war to reach a new state of nuclear safety quickly, but entails a risk that the process will be derailed. Once again, however, cooperative engagement might achieve results not possible in the traditional arms control framework. Presidents Bush and Yeltsin appear to have recognized this possibility when they suggested that with U.S. assistance, implementation of the START follow-on agreement might be completed by 2000 rather than 2003.

An example of such a cooperative approach would be to attempt to forge cooperative agreements that focused on warheads instead of launchers. An important precedent for this approach was the September 1991 reciprocal unilateral initiative covering tactical nuclear weapons, wherein the United States and the then–Soviet Union pledged to withdraw many thousands of tactical warheads from active service and to dismantle many of them. An analogous scheme for strategic weapons would allow the security benefits of the START agreement and the follow-on framework agreement to be achieved well before 2003. The parties could agree to the immediate removal of the warheads from all launchers slated for eventual deactivation under these agreements.

Judging from the pace at which tactical nuclear weapons were removed from active service to central storage depots by both sides since September 1991, removal of strategic warheads could probably be accomplished in less than a year. Such a bold form of denuclearization would extend the process begun with tactical nuclear weapons to strategic weapons. It would remove the danger of unauthorized or accidental launch of weapons covered by the agreements, since launch would be harmless if the delivery vehicles had no warheads. It would accomplish in one year the removal of all nuclear warheads from Ukraine, Kazakhstan, and Belarus, heading off any possibility of nuclear proliferation in the former Soviet Union. It would dramatically underscore the deemphasizing of nuclear weapons that is so much in the interests of the great powers. Though not verifiable by cold war standards, a cooperative scheme could probably be arranged that would give all parties adequate confidence that their security was not being compromised. In any event, warhead removal would be reversible in the short term, and thus warheads could be reloaded if the process bogged down.

A focus on nuclear warheads leads in turn to other fruitful avenues of nuclear cooperation. Both the United States and Russia possess inventories of nuclear weapons five to ten times the size they project for deployment in ten years. The surplus weapons need to be dismantled, plutonium and enriched uranium produced for weapons need to be eliminated or stored, and the nuclear weapons complexes need to be environmentally cleaned up and restructured for their post–cold war role of supporting smaller and simpler arsenals. All these tasks are appropriate for cooperative effort. Indeed, some cooperation is probably a prerequisite for sustaining political support for denuclearization in each country. And in Russia, U.S. assistance might stimulate and hasten actions that would otherwise take place much more slowly, or not at all, because of lack of money and because they would not otherwise receive high priority amidst the many needs of a society in social and economic stress. Finally, an ongoing internationally sanctioned process of nuclear builddown in Russia is probably a prerequisite for Ukraine, Kazakhstan, and Belarus to resist any temptation to try to stake a claim to nuclear weapons based on their territory.

The needed cooperation does not end with the United States and the states of the former Soviet Union. In at least two facets of denuclearization, broader international cooperation is desirable and perhaps necessary. The first is disposing of fissile materials from dismantled weapons and accumulated stocks of weapons grade plutonium and enriched uranium. Both of these materials have half-lives of many thousands of years and no alternative use except as fuel for nuclear power reactors. The market for uranium reactor fuels is global, and several states—notably Britain, France, and Japan—are involved in actual or planned use of plutonium. These states will inevitably play a role in any use of weapons materials for reactor fuels. It is probably even desirable for the international community to assume long-term custody of weapons grade materials after denuclearization has taken place in the United States and Russia. Indeed, as noted, internationalizing the process of denuclearization might be the only way to bring the states of the former Soviet Union to agreement on completing it. Finally, broader international participation in denuclearization might prove to be a first exploratory step toward bringing the British, French, and Chinese nuclear arsenals into negotiated arms control—a task that virtually everyone concedes is logically inevitable but no one knows quite how to approach.

If all goes as planned in this historical process of denuclearization, the total inventory of some 55,000 nuclear weapons that was the legacy of cold war with the former Soviet Union will have shrunk to some 10,000 weapons in the arsenals of Russia and the United States by the end of the century or soon thereafter. This builddown will accomplish much toward nuclear safety. But nuclear arsenals need to be made safer as well as smaller.

Important steps toward safety, security, and control of nuclear forces can be taken, once again, cooperatively. Traditionally, cooperative pursuit of nuclear safety has been mainly through enhancing "strategic stability," that is, arranging for each side to have the capability for hefty retaliation to a nuclear first strike with high assurance under all conceivable circumstances. This is a worthy, indeed indispensable, ingredient of nuclear safety. It was pursued with extraordinary energy by both sides in the cold war, through unilateral deployments and through cooperation in arms control. Actions by either side that could be interpreted as upsetting retaliatory stability, for instance, the Soviet SS-18 heavy missile or the U.S. strategic defense initiative, became the bones of contention at the negotiating table.

But retaliatory stability was usually pursued much more vigorously, and sometimes at the price of what might be called operational stability: not only should retaliation be assured and hefty, but the operations that the nuclear forces must undertake to survive attack and mount retaliation should themselves be safe. Here the cold war record is much poorer. Hasty retaliatory timelines (including provision for retaliation to begin before the provoking attack was even over, and accepting force and command and control configurations that could not accomplish retaliation if orders were delayed too long), dependence on strategic or tactical warning of attack, and subtle interdependencies among legs of the strategic triad (for instance, the supposed dependence of bombers and ICBMs on each other for launch on tactical warning, or the dependence of bombers on precursor missile attacks on opposing air defense installations for their penetration of enemy airspace) were accepted in the pursuit of ever more weighty and assured retaliation.

The nuclear arsenals after denuclearization should not only exhibit retaliatory stability, but operational stability. The goal should be not only the capability for weighty and assured retaliation, but freedom from dependence on alerting and warning, and above all, freedom from reliance on prompt response. Peacetime and alert operations should reemphasize safety and control over readiness—or, in common parlance, negative control over positive control.

Operational stability would be furthered by several steps, all of which could be pursued cooperatively. One focus of such cooperation would be survivability of command and control systems, which have always been the not-so-hidden Achilles' heels of the superpower strategic arsenals, emphasizing mutual restraints on capabilities for surprise attack or specialized means of attack on command and control systems, including antisatellites. Another focus would be cooperative restraints covering alerting procedures and nuclear exercises. A third would be cooperative systems for missile warning, such as Russia and the United States have proposed. Cooperation could even go so far as to permit each side to install warning sensors in the missile silo fields of the other. Finally, a decisive tilt toward negative control would call for installation of the most modern technical safeguards (often called permissive action links or PALs) on all nuclear weapons remaining in the inventory. Such devices should permit physical enabling of weapons only by the highest authorities. Such enabling should also be selective, so that it can be applied to any subset of the arsenal without "unlocking" the rest; contingent, so that unlocked weapons could only be used against intended targets; and reversible, so that unlocked weapons could be locked up again.

At the end of the cold war, it is therefore possible to envision a dramatic deemphasis of the role of nuclear weapons in security, smaller and simplified arsenals, and enhanced safety and security—all pursued cooperatively. Though logic might suggest them, these processes will not occur easily on either side unless the other is seen to be undergoing similar change. The ongoing revolution in the former Soviet Union furthermore poses an entirely new security calculus for the United States: the price of failure to induce a graceful and controlled process of denuclearization would not just be a historic opportunity lost, but possibly a disaster.

This dramatic denuclearization pending among the great powers may well have a salutary effect on the thinking about nuclear weapons in other parts of the world, and thus on proliferation. Nuclear have-nots and aspirants have always claimed that horizontal proliferation could not be controlled unless vertical proliferation came under control. Among the nuclear "haves," many have suspected that this claim merely provided a convenient cover for attitudes toward proliferation that were actually determined by regional security dilemmas and internal politics among the nations considered to be proliferation risks. But the claim was never put to the test. Now it should be.

Vertical proliferation is undergoing a dramatic reversal. Though a comprehensive ban on underground nuclear testing, which has frequently been taken to symbolize control over vertical proliferation, is not yet part of the agreed denuclearization agenda between the United States and the former Soviet Union, that omission warrants only a footnote in view of the fivefold or so reductions in warhead inventories and major cutbacks in arsenal modernization planned by the United States and Russia. The signatories of the Nuclear Nonproliferation Treaty meet in 1995 to consider whether to renew this important agreement or allow it to lapse. The transformation of superpower arsenals and thinking about nuclear weapons can and should influence their deliberations.

Deemphasis of nuclear weapons in the military doctrines of the great powers might reinforce abhorrence and rejection of nuclear weapons around the world. Steps to enhance safety, security, and control set an example of sober, responsible custodianship. International control of the disposition of weapons grade plutonium and enriched uranium would strengthen the global regime of control on nuclear materials. More directly, failure of denuclearization in the former Soviet Union would clearly have a negative effect on nonproliferation, if any of the non-Russian successor states fails to carry out its pledge to be nuclear weapons–free, or if sensitive materials, know-how, or weapons are diverted.

Thus relegation of nuclear weapons to a background role in international security, reduction of active arsenals and dismantlement of the surplus, enhancement of the safety of remaining weapons, and nonproliferation are all becoming parts of one security problem. Solutions to that problem must be cooperative.

Defensive Configuration of Conventional Forces

If defense of national territory is the sole purpose of nationally controlled military forces, then they should be so configured that they cannot be readily dislodged from their home territory but also cannot effectively attack anyone else's. That implication provides a natural standard for regulating the allowed size and peacetime operations of conventional forces, but it also presents immediate practical difficulties. The distinction between offensive and defensive capability cannot be clearly drawn in physical terms. Nearly all weapons can support offensive or defensive purposes depending on how they are utilized. Overall defensive and offensive force configurations are not discrete categories but a continuous spectrum, and the determination of where any given military deployment might fall on that spectrum involves judgments about firepower, weapons mix, operational doctrine, training history, and underlying intention. Such judgments cannot be reduced to a formula that would withstand analytic dispute and political suspicion.

Moreover, the scope and the apparent incentive for dispute over such limits are substantial. In order to align the existing military establishments with a defensive standard, it appears that prevailing operational doctrines would have to be reversed or at least severely contained. Although the major military establishments assertively and sincerely declare their defensive intentions, over recent decades their technological development and operational planning have come to emphasize rapidly executed deep interdiction missions against an opponent's organizational structure rather than its frontline firepower. These doctrines, which are believed to be dictated by the technical imperatives of modern warfare, invariably rely on surprise and strongly encourage preemption. They have the politically appealing effect of displacing much of the destruction caused by one's own forces onto the opponent's territory and the emotionally appealing effect of justifying strong initiative and bold military leadership. And they have been demonstrated to be effective, most notably in the recent Persian Gulf War. Effective implementation of the principle of defensive configuration contests this tradition and demands revisions that are not incremental in character. A revolution in military practice seems to be required.

To compound this difficulty, the revolution also seems particularly difficult to justify for two of the leading cases. The U.S. military establishment, which currently possesses the most advanced capacity for global power projection, experiences no contiguous military threat to its home territory. There is no need for large military forces in the continental United States, and most of their value would be forfeited if they could not be projected to geographically remote situations. Israeli military forces, which have superior power projection capabilities in the most turbulent region of the world, are driven by a different calculus to a similar operational commitment. The military posture of the Israelis is designed to defend a small amount of territory against a number of contiguous states that are perceived to be intensely hostile and that in the aggregate outnumber them. Unwilling to risk any penetration of their limited space, Israeli military forces have developed a doctrine of rapid mobilization and preemptive offense that is deeply ingrained and would be very difficult to redirect.

If the most capable military establishments appear at the outset to be so intractable, then even those countries whose security requirements are most compatible with a defensive configuration of forces—notably Russia and China—might be reluctant to accept a defensive configuration as an international standard. Fortunately, however, a practical arrangement can achieve the essential purposes of defensive configuration without indisputably exact measurement or a radical reversal of prevailing operational doctrine. The situation is less intractable than it seems at first.

There is a major advantage in the fact that seizing territory and establishing political control over it requires large ground force movements. With advanced reconnaissance methods, preparations for ground assaults are extremely difficult to conceal, and cooperative rules could readily make tactical surprise impossible. And tactical air operations, which now provide the decisive elements of a successful preemptive offensive, are dependent on coordinated air traffic control. Internationalizing the function of military air traffic control offers a practical means of imposing a meaningful buffer between normal peacetime activity and the preemptive air operations that would initiate an aggressive war.

The key to such international control would be the creation of an international surveillance system that maintained a current "order of battle" of military aircraft on a worldwide basis. Such a surveillance system, to be effective, would have to consist of continuous, routine inputs from three and possibly four generic subsystems: the extensive system of ground-based radars in the international civil air traffic control network, international inspectors established in the manner of CSCE, the satellite reconnaissance systems employed by several nations, most notably the United States, and possible new internationally developed and operated space reconnaissance systems. The creation of such an information system would require the solution of at least two problems: the distillation, transmission, and synthesis of data from the extensive air traffic control network to some central control station and the declassification and transmission to this control station of certain data from the nationally controlled satellite systems, so these data could be integrated with the air traffic control data.

By imposing controls on the location and movement of ground forces in peacetime and on tactical air operations, a practical cooperative arrangement can keep national military establishments disengaged from immediate confrontation and unable to make the extensive preparations necessary to mount a ground force offensive without triggering international reactions. However, even with such controls, it is possible to envision preemptive, surprise attacks of strike aircraft when the distance separating the opposing nations is as short as it is in the Mideast and when the strike aircraft are kept in shelters until shortly before the attack. Therefore the control mechanism must include the threat of sanctions, which, as a last resort, would entail an internationally organized air attack that could very credibly promise to disrupt the intricate coordination required to sustain a successful ground offensive. That strategy of control concentrates restrictions on the most vulnerable part of an offensive operation—ground force movements—and seeks to appropriate the most capable part—tactical air operations—to defend the cooperative arrangement against any major challenge. The strategy also implies the availability of the U.S. reconnaissance strike complex capability to the international forces executing the military sanctions.

A successful ground offensive normally requires that a significant firepower advantage be brought to bear at the point of attack in order to dislodge the defending force. In order to seize territory, an offensive force has to move and thereby expose itself more than the defending force that can operate from concealed and protected positions. That usually results in higher attrition rates for the offensive force in competitively contested battles. A firepower advantage is necessary to offset the higher expected rate of attrition and to make the offensive succeed. Cooperative control provisions covering ground forces should therefore seek to equalize available firepower and to prevent unbalanced concentration at any point of potential attack.

Since sovereign countries have substantially different amounts of territory to defend, different-sized populations, and different military traditions, exact equality on each frontier is not a feasible aspiration. It is possible to imagine, however, common standards for the density of forces (a standard military unit for a given territorial perimeter to be defended); concentration (the force allowed to be assembled at any given location); movement (the force allowed to be moved from one location to another in a given time); and transparency (basic information about force size, location, movement, and rates of investment provided to the international community). If international rules were established in these terms, the major ground force establishments could be set in configurations that are reasonably accepted as defensive. The precise details would matter less than the fact that common rules were defined and enforced, and that they were accompanied by extensive transparency.

While a comprehensive set of military force restraints has never been established on a global basis, the precursor of such a global set of restraints on ground and air forces can be seen clearly in Europe. The CFE agreement imposes national ceilings on ground force equipment (tanks, armored personnel carriers, and artillery pieces) and tactical aircraft and helicopters. These ceilings, while not derived from a requirement to make all national borders defensible but rather to restrict the offensive potential of the former Eastern and Western alliances, nonetheless go a long way toward establishing the principle of defensive postures in Europe. The extensive CSBMs established by the CSCE in 1990, which restrict the peacetime movement and concentration of the armies limited by the CFE, also further constrain offensive potential. The Open Skies agreement, together with the inspections that are part of the CFE and the CSBMs, establishes a higher standard of transparency. Finally, negotiations are under way to provide integrated air traffic control over the whole of Europe.

Major ingredients of a cooperative security regime therefore already exist in Europe. This evolving regime provides all states with a reassuring cap on the threat from their neighbors. It furnishes an internationally shared rationale for the economically and socially disruptive process of rapid demobilization faced by all European governments. It establishes a cooperative benchmark for the size and structure of their military establishments for new states emerging from the former Soviet Union that are defining their security postures, as well as for old states realigning their postures to their post–cold war situation. It establishes a framework in which violators of the rules or the peace are sanctioned and—less directly but importantly—it establishes a habit of cooperative engagement among military establishments that makes collective security peacekeeping operations more likely to succeed when needed. Continuing to build this European web of restraint, and extending it to other regions, with suitable adjustment for their special needs, is a principal aim of cooperative security.

Internationalized Response to Aggression

Most security relationships throughout the world would be decisively stabilized by common rules that restrict national military forces to a defensive configuration and even the difficult cases would become less dangerous. Nonetheless even the most exacting rules would have too much ambiguity to carry the full burden of international security. Clever exploitation of the common rules, variations in geography that make defense more difficult for some countries than others, and the possibility of a rogue nation secretly developing an offensive capability in violation of the rules would provide some scope for aggression. Therefore an integral part of any cooperative security regime must be the capability to organize multinational forces to defeat aggression should it occur. This capacity would provide a background deterrent effect as well as physical protection. The United Nations Security Council can authorize multinational military forces for this purpose;

indeed, the U.N. is authorized to form its own military force. It is more immediately realistic, however, to focus on U.N. authorization of multinational forces to deal with major acts of aggression on an ad hoc basis.

In a cooperative security regime, the use of military force by the United Nations—or any nation—is a last resort, to be invoked only after political pressure and economic sanctions have failed. The threat of military force should be sufficient to obviate the need to use it if the right military and political conditions are met. The threat will be maximally effective when political conditions permit the military force to be a broadly based coalition.

This broad international support makes the U.N. threat of military action politically credible. The threat also will be militarily credible if the coalition military force is organized around the reconnaissance strike complex employed by the United States in Desert Storm. Organizing the force around conventional armored combined forces could lead to a long and bloody ground war, and an aggressor might believe that he could wear down the resolve of the coalition governments (as Saddam Hussein believed at the beginning of the Gulf War). Organizing the threat of military force around nuclear weapons would not be credible, particularly if the aggressor had some nuclear weapons of his own. Nuclear nations in a cooperative security regime must maintain a sufficient nuclear capability that no aggressor nation could ever see an advantage by initiating a nuclear attack; on the other hand, they should not regard their nuclear weapons as a deterrent to aggression with conventional weapons.

In any multinational military force organized around a reconnaissance strike complex, the United States military would have a special role to play. It would provide most of the airlift required to quickly transport coalition military forces to the theater; it would provide most of the tactical intelligence data required to support the precision strike weapons; and it would supply most of the stealth aircraft used to suppress enemy air defenses. On the other hand, coalition partners would participate on an equal basis in achieving air and naval superiority in the theater, and would play a dominant role in the ground forces of the coalition. In this view of cooperative security, the special military capability of the United States would be used to give coalition forces an advantage that not only insured a military victory, but one that could be achieved with minimal losses to coalition forces. Therefore it should provide maximum deterrent to any potential aggressor.

Precisely because of the great deterrent effect of this military capability, any potential aggressor would be seeking ways to defeat it. Therefore we should expect to see efforts to emulate it, efforts to finesse it, and efforts to counter it. This capability could indeed be emulated by a half dozen of the advanced industrial nations of the world, but at great expense and with a very visible effort. It is unlikely to be emulated by any of the regional powers that we presently consider to be potential aggressors.

A more likely strategy for a potential aggressor is to try to finesse this military capability by developing weapons of mass destruction, especially nuclear weapons. While this response would be essentially suicidal, an aggressor might convince itself that it could succeed in such a bluff—certainly the self-destructive actions of Iraq suggest that Saddam Hussein was basing much of his strategy on bluffs or gross misconceptions about the resolve of coalition nations. Therefore a cooperative security regime should place a very high priority on actions designed to prevent the proliferation of weapons of mass destruction, especially nuclear weapons. Another possible strategy for a potential aggressor is to develop countermeasures to the reconnaissance strike force, which can be done to some degree by many nations. This prospect suggests that the United States should dedicate a portion of its defense effort to appropriate counter-countermeasures.

More generally, the United States would require a major restructuring and downsizing of its defense forces under a cooperative security regime. Such restructuring would have three major objectives:

a. to effect a significant reduction in the size of U.S. ground and naval forces (with a concomitant reduction in the defense budget). The new ground and naval forces would be sized to deal with credible military threats to U.S. territory; to provide the cadre for reconstitution of U.S. forces if a new superpower military threat emerged (that is, if the cooperative security regime collapsed); and to provide whatever (minimal) ground and naval support the United States might be requested to provide to multinational military forces;

b. to maintain a capability to provide a core contribution to the strategic intelligence evaluations that assess the emergence of new threats to the cooperative security regime, as well as key inputs to the verification of treaties or U.N. sanctions (limits on weapon developments or force deployments, for example); and

c. to maintain a capability to provide key elements of the reconnaissance strike military forces that would be used in multinational military actions whenever diplomacy and economic sanctions proved to be insufficient.

Other nations belonging to the cooperative security regime would also restructure and downsize their defense forces. Their objectives in restructuring would be conceptually similar to the objectives of the United States, but these objectives would manifest themselves in different ways depending on their circumstances. Objective (a) would be the same for all members of the regime. For some of these nations, providing for their territorial defense would involve maintaining significant ground forces. Russia, Germany, France, China, and India, for example, would have the bulk of the ground forces, and would therefore be expected to make up the bulk of the ground forces needed in any multinational expeditionary force. Similarly, the United Kingdom, Italy, and Japan would place a greater emphasis on naval forces for their territorial defense and would therefore make the major contributions to the naval arm of a multinational force. Only a few nations besides the United States (Russia and the United Kingdom, for example) have developed and deployed global strategic intelligence assets that permit them to make a significant contribution to global threat evaluation and verification assessment (Objective (b)). These nations would be expected to make such a contribution to the appropriate international coalition. A handful of nations have military capabilities that would be of special importance to the reconnaissance strike force (Objective (c)). Russia has significant capability in airlift, sealift, and air superiority aircraft; France, Germany, and the United Kingdom have a significant capability in air superiority aircraft. Therefore these nations, along with the United States, would provide the reconnaissance strike elements of any multinational expeditionary force.

Thus, in the interest of maintaining the power projection capability needed when major military actions must be undertaken by the cooperative security regime, some nations will end up with national defense forces larger than needed for territorial defense. This asymmetry will likely cause two related political problems. Some nations will fear that the nations with the larger defense forces will apply their military forces to achieve national or hegemonic objectives. Others will fear that the nations with the larger forces will let this special military capability erode or be reluctant to use it, so that it will not be available when needed for multinational forces. Each of these fears has some historical justification; indeed, both could be realized at the same time.

Thus a substantial challenge for a cooperative security regime would be to work out the political measures that minimize these risks. For example, the nations with the reconnaissance strike forces could establish dual command channels (analogous to those established in NATO for nuclear weapons) for these forces. Also, the U.N. could establish funding to assist in the maintenance of certain of these national forces. Finally, the nations with these special forces could agree not to use them in violation of the U.N. charter.

As difficult as it will be to meet these political challenges, the two logical alternatives are even less attractive. One alternative is for the United States, for example, to disband its airlift and reconnaissance strike forces, since arguably they are not needed for territorial defense. However, this would greatly weaken the ability of any multinational force to decisively defeat a military threat posed by an aggressor nation with sizable armored forces. The other alternative would be for the United States and other relevant nations to turn over these special forces to the U.N., giving the U.N. a large (several hundred thousand men) permanent military force. For a variety of reasons, such a move would probably be impractical to implement. In any event, the U.N. would probably be better served with a relatively small permanent military force, designed for peacekeeping duties, as proposed by the present secretary general. Peacekeeping U.N. forces would likely be called into action many times. The special expeditionary force would be assembled only on an ad hoc basis, and this would occur rarely if the cooperative security regime is effective.

If this rationale for defense restructuring were followed, the United States would have special requirements in its defense modernization to maintain and enhance the reconnaissance strike capability that would be called on by the multinational force. While these units were remarkably effective in operations against the large and well-equipped Iraqi army, the world has seen their effectiveness, so it is reasonable to assume that any potential aggressor would understand that he would need to develop some plausible way of countering this capability before he could act. The world has also seen certain weaknesses in the reconnaissance strike forces used in Desert Storm—indeed, the United States has publicly described some of the vulnerabilities of these systems. To be sure, these were "latent" vulnerabilities that the Iraqis failed to exploit, but prudent planning should assume that a future aggressor would try to take full advantage of these vulnerabilities.

Therefore, in order to maintain the effectiveness of this critical capability, the United States should embark on a program to overcome the vulnerabilities of its present systems to countermeasures.

As it was used in Desert Storm, the U.S. reconnaissance strike complex consisted of three primary elements: C^3I (Command, Control, Communications, and Intelligence), defense suppression, and precision-guided munitions (PGMs). The first of the critical components is C^3I. In Desert Storm the United States used reconnaissance satellites, which were developed originally for national intelligence, for combat support, employed AWACS to get a continuous order-of-battle of all air vehicles, and for the first time used a system called JSTARS for a continuous order-of-battle of all ground vehicles. U.S. forces made extensive use of night vision, as well as global positioning satellites to locate forces on the ground. All of this gave coalition commanders superb "situation awareness"; that is, they knew precisely where enemy forces were located, where friendly forces were located, and where they themselves were located. At the same time, very early in that campaign, coalition forces essentially destroyed the Iraqi C^3I system.

Precision-guided munitions comprised the second critical component of the reconnaissance strike force. In Desert Storm, the F-117 dropped 2,100 laser-guided bombs and of these, 1,700 landed within ten feet of the designated aim point, thereby destroying the targets that they were attacking. There is no precedent for that sort of performance in any previous use of air power, and this remarkable effectiveness played a critical role in the rapid defeat of the Iraqi forces.

Defense suppression was a third critical component. The Iraqis had a modern, dense, netted, hardened air defense system, which was especially dense around Baghdad. Historically, air defenses with that capability have inflicted attrition losses of 1 to 2 percent on attacking forces. With the 3,000 sorties a day conducted by coalition air forces, a 1 to 2 percent attrition rate would have resulted in the loss of 30 to 60 airplanes each day, and over a 30-day campaign, 1,000 to 2,000 airplanes. Instead of losing 30 to 60 airplanes a day, the coalition lost about 1 per day. This was a result of the introduction of Stealth (the F-117 and the Tomahawk missile) and the use of antiradiation missiles. The combined effectiveness of these three weapons systems essentially destroyed the Iraqi air defense electronics subsystems. As a consequence, that air defense did not have radar or command and control, and they were left simply with guns that they could fire visually or in a barrage, which resulted in about one-thirtieth of 1 percent attrition.

Equally important to the effectiveness of the reconnaissance strike force was the synergism among these three components. The effectiveness of the defense suppression weapons depended on the precision-guided munitions. The effectiveness of the precision-guided munitions depended on the reconnaissance systems for targeting. The very survivability of the reconnaissance systems depended on the effectiveness of defense suppression.

Thus the decisive factor in this war was the application of this new defense technology, especially the truly extraordinary application of air power deployed in a "system of systems." At present, the United States is the only nation that has this full spectrum of capabilities, and this will continue to be true for the foreseeable future. Therefore, in order for a cooperative security regime to have the military force that can credibly threaten multinational military action if its diplomatic initiatives or economic sanctions fail, the United States must maintain this capability in the face of plausible countermeasures, and the United States must be willing to make these forces available as their contribution to multinational forces whenever military action is necessary. The primary objective of having such a military capability, of course, is to make the threat of military force so credible that it will never have to be used. Iraq persisted in its defiance of U.N. orders, not because it believed that it could defeat the coalition forces, but because it believed that it could force a long and bloody war on them (as in Vietnam), which would create the conditions for a diplomatic victory.

Restraints on Military Investment and Proliferation

Cooperative standards for the overall size of ground forces and tactical air forces would be a political convenience rather than an imposed burden for most military establishments. Most are already affected by competing economic priorities and by a growing realization that the projection of military power cannot be the dominant instrument of policy. The dissolution of an immediate sense of threat and corresponding domestic budget restrictions are very likely to shrink the major military establishments to levels more compatible with standards of cooperative security. That prospect gives the establishments an incentive to formalize those standards and induce compliance by others.

However, domestic politics do not provide the same natural restriction on longer-term patterns of investment in military technology and the directly related problem of weapons proliferation. International cooperative regulation would therefore have greater consequence and would carry a heavier political burden.

Historically the major military establishments have imposed virtually no restraint (other than budgetary) on their own efforts at technical development and have accepted the proliferation of weapons technology as a consequence. They have competed in the development of advanced weapons in pursuit of a national comparative advantage to be realized over periods of five to ten years. Since it was believed that a major war might occur during those spans of time and that technical advantage might be decisive, the longer-term effects of technical diffusion were subordinate considerations. Formal efforts were made to control proliferation of weapons, especially weapons of mass destruction, but these were not the primary focus of security. In fact, the United States, the Soviet Union, the United Kingdom, and France all actively promoted the sale of advanced conventional weapons as an instrument of foreign policy and as a means of offsetting the unit cost of these weapons for their own military forces.

As a result, proliferation controls have been fragmented, incompletely developed, and poorly coordinated. Moreover, the relentless worldwide extension of knowledge, technology, and advanced manufacturing processes and specialty materials has undermined the principal policy mechanisms used for control—security classification and export licensing. These mechanisms no longer govern access by any of the advanced industrial countries or by others with adequate resources to trade with the industrialized countries.

This endemic problem of proliferation control is powerfully reinforced by trends in the worldwide diffusion of technology, assuring that restraint in acquiring destructive weapons must be induced through cooperation rather than compelled through denial of access. One trend, now nearly fully realized, is the equalization of technical potential among the Western industrialized nations. This equalization is clearest in commercial technology rather than in purely military technology. But although U.S. military systems are superior to corresponding British, French, and German systems in general, exceptions occur. Some export versions of non-U.S. weapons can clearly pose a threat to U.S. forces even though they are not necessarily as sophisticated as their U.S. equivalents. The French Exocet sea-skimming antiship cruise missile and, more palpably, technologies that can contribute to weapons of mass destruction are examples. A deepening relationship between military and commercial technology also suggests that equivalence in commercial technology will increasingly affect military technology.

Technological equalization among the Western industrialized nations is obviously not a new trend, and for some technologies, such as nuclear power, it has long been a fact. But today's huge international trade in technology opens up many opportunities and avenues for illicit diversions of technology that can affect proliferation. It creates compelling economic stakes for all the Western nations in capturing and maintaining foreign markets, in turn creating political obstacles to proliferation controls. It fosters heated competition among firms and nations, tempting all to cut nonproliferation corners to secure access to markets. In short, it makes it absolutely imperative to secure the concurrence of all the advanced nations in any proliferation control strategy that can possibly be effective.

More narrowly but still important, equalization will probably enhance the perception of threat from proliferation among the military establishments of the advanced nations, especially the United States. The Pentagon has long been accustomed to facing Soviet weapons in the hands of Soviet clients in regional conflicts. But the Soviets were usually careful about the sophistication of the technology they sold abroad. In any event Soviet-made weapons were precisely those against which U.S. weapons were engineered and U.S. forces trained, so the American military was prepared for them with thorough intelligence and a full array of tailored military responses. But in the future, U.S. forces will face weapons manufactured in Western Europe that are highly sophisticated and largely unfamiliar.

As military leaders recognize this trend, proliferation will more often be treated as a mainstream military threat rather than merely a diplomatic problem. Indeed, the Gulf War stimulated some recognition of this kind. Iraq's air defense system, though largely of Soviet design, had important components supplied from Europe. The U.S. Navy was forced to pay inordinate attention to the threat from French Exocet missiles. And much of the dense and redundant Iraqi command and control system that the planners of the U.S. bombing campaign were so intent on destroying was of state-of-the-art Western design.

A second trend is the rising technical capability of the less developed nations. They accept easily and are reassured by the thought that an aspiring proliferator—say, North Korea—is "forty years behind the

United States" in technology. But in 1953 the United States was eight years beyond having obtained nuclear weapons indigenously, was stockpiling chemical and biological weapons not much different from those that would be deemed technically "optimal" on the basis of today's biological and chemical knowledge, and was well on its way toward acquiring intercontinental jet bomber and missile fleets.

Today's commonly available commercial technology can also be startling when placed in historical context. The efficient, varied, high yield-to-weight-ratio thermonuclear weapons attained by the United States by the 1960s were designed through the use of computers with less computational power than a handful of today's laptop personal computers (PCs), and with a good deal less computational power than a low-end workstation.

Related to the rising tide of technological sophistication is the emergence of a second tier of suppliers of weapons and of technology for weapons of mass destruction. Thirty years ago it was possible to formulate the proliferation control problem by reference to three blocs of critical suppliers: the United States, the Western industrialized nations, and the Soviet Union. In the intervening years an expanded base of supply has taken root and now dominates the problem of control. The expanded base consists of China, India, newly industrialized nations of the Pacific rim, North Korea, Israel, South Africa, Brazil, Argentina, and the states of the former Soviet bloc, including the new states emerging from the former Soviet Union. A number of these states are themselves "of concern" for proliferation. Many new suppliers began their weapons programs through cooperative developments with defense firms in the advanced industrialized world, gradually increasing their own technological capabilities until they could produce weapons independently.

Today such nations can pool technology and talent among themselves in joint development programs, and they can cooperate with one another in illicit diversions of technology and in illicit weapons development programs. Though most in the expanded base cooperate in nonproliferation efforts, many feel they have little stake in control-through-denial strategies orchestrated by the advanced nations, and most of those nations resent such strategies as discriminatory. In some cases the establishment of a military technology base funded in part by foreign sales is a part of the nation's strategy for civil, economic, and technological development. Their insistence on their fair market share in the international arms trade, and their growing desperation as the arms markets in many parts of the world shrink, means that they will not cooperate in control strategies they do not consider equitable.

Associated with the emergence of an expanded base of suppliers is the appearance of joint development programs among proliferators and truly global networks of supply for advanced weapons technology. Cooperative development programs are commonplace. Aspiring proliferators are forming partnerships, as in the celebrated Condor missile collaboration of Argentina, Iraq, and Egypt. Less advanced nations, when entering into arrangements to acquire uncontrolled weapons from advanced countries, are frequently demanding that the supplier transfer technology, as well as end items. This is accomplished by building production plants in the recipient country or by subcontracting component production to the recipient country, thereby strengthening the recipient's military technology base. Even when international supply networks involve relatively innocuous types of military equipment, they establish a style that can be followed by illicit programs and a body of unobjectionable commerce and technical activity in which illicit activity can be concealed.

It is no longer possible for control strategies to focus on simple donor-recipient pairs. In the past the erosion of proliferation regimes usually took that form. Today the supply networks frequently include several collaborating parties, parallel efforts to obtain technology through different channels, and transshipment of illicit goods through one or two intermediate stops. These developments make it much more difficult for control to focus on individual "problem" states or problem transactions. Such focus on individual links in the network of supply has characterized much of the episodic and ad hoc nonproliferation effort that has resulted from the routine subordination of proliferation control to other security, economic, and political objectives. The appearance of global networks of supply means that attempts to focus control efforts narrowly and episodically will fail.

As mentioned earlier, yet another trend in technology that profoundly affects proliferation is the changing relationship between military and civil technology. Technology of importance to military systems now often originates in the commercial sector, and research and development performed by commercial firms more often dominates and drives the evolution of defense technology. These developments in turn place much of the technical activity important to nonproliferation outside of the control of security agencies and defense industries and squarely in the mainstream of commerce.

Finally, the economic crisis in the former Soviet Union also affects proliferation. Capitalizing the needed process of conversion is widely believed by industry managers and political leaders in the former Soviet Union to require hard-currency export sales of military equipment. Although the potential export markets that the defense firms of the former Soviet Union might capture are probably not, in fact, nearly large enough in aggregate to provide the capital that is needed for conversion, hopes run high among industry managers. Thus the pressures to sell abroad are even greater for them than for Western firms.

Moreover, political controls in the nations of the former Soviet Union are weak in the midst of their ongoing political and economic revolutions. Export control legislation is incomplete. Surveillance and enforcement mechanisms are weak. Faced with dire economic straits, nonproliferation probably seems a remote and abstract concern to many economic and political leaders. Defense industry managers find themselves burdened with work forces facing massive layoffs with no prospect of a renewal of domestic orders. An "auction" of the high-technology cold war legacy of the former Soviet Union is thus a real possibility. Even though Soviet products might be regarded as inferior by potential buyers around the world because of the admitted "failure" of communism and the perceived success of Western arms in the Gulf War, their easy availability and low price will probably attract buyers. And though this technological trend affecting proliferation is recent and sudden, it will have long-lasting effects because the economic underdevelopment of the former Soviet Union will not be altered soon.

All of these trends point in the same direction, namely, toward increased access to weapons technology by states—or by ministries or factions within states—bent on proliferation. Furthermore, technology is not only becoming more freely available, but the paths through which it is made available increasingly involve complex networks of partners rather than simple donor-recipient pairs. Thus control becomes an inherently multinational, indeed international, undertaking. These trends have been widely noted and are, to a certain extent, widely understood to profoundly affect the control of proliferation. But the full weight of the threat they pose to prevailing control strategies, singly and even more urgently when considered together, has not been reflected in the enactment of new policies.

It is important to emphasize that the trends described above are not fully realized: they are trends, not completed metamorphoses. They apply in different degrees to different weapons types. They do not make the proliferation control strategies of the cold war era completely obsolete. These strategies were based largely on denying aspiring proliferators the technical capabilities to realize their aspirations. This denial was furthermore to be exercised by the few advanced industrial nations with the technological potential to contribute to proliferation, and within those nations by relatively few firms. But these trends do call into question very strongly the future viability of those control strategies. They suggest that strategy based on denial of access and orchestrated by the advanced industrial nations will fail in time—and for some nations and some weapons types is failing already. This looming failure is a strong motivation to take cooperative security seriously.

The new security situation thus dictates a decisive shift in priority. The pursuit of national comparative advantage must be subordinated to the control of proliferation. Accompanying this shift should be a change in the principal mechanisms of control from denial of access to cooperatively induced restraint. Controlling access to information and materials remains feasible and important for some of the critical components of nuclear weapons that can be segregated from commercial markets. But for chemical and biological agents, conventional munitions and advanced delivery system technology, and for the command and control systems that spell the difference in modern warfare, basic access to the underlying technology and components cannot be effectively denied. These systems are not as affected by the natural inhibitions and historical taboos associated with the tremendous destructive power of nuclear weapons. But they pose a serious problem of control and require a control strategy focused more on the application of technology than on access to it—more, therefore, on intentions than on technical capabilities.

In order to have any reasonable hope of inducing restraint among the many countries that have the inherent capacity and potential incentive to acquire advanced weapons, the major military establishments would not only have to subordinate their own national forces to international coalitions, as described above, but also would undoubtedly have to shrink reciprocally their own forces, levels, and defense industries and would probably have to adopt deployment restrictions embodying the principles of defensive configuration. They would also have to radically deemphasize weapons of mass destruction in their defense planning. Fortunately, historic contractions in military forces and investment of just this sort are taking place throughout North America, Europe, and the former Soviet Union. If carried out cooperatively, this contraction can set the standard for reduced military spending and for force and investment cuts in other regions. Contraction in defense industries and control of export sales should be transformed from politically charged national burdens into internationally shared obligations in pursuit of the benefit of lower levels of militarization everywhere.

Indeed, as discussed, the major powers are deemphasizing nuclear weapons. If the U.S. and Russian nuclear arsenals were further reduced cooperatively to say 2,000 warheads each and the British, Chinese, and French forces to 500 each, one might imagine that existing arrangements for preventing nuclear proliferation would be sufficiently buttressed to preserve their effectiveness. One might also believe that the completion of the treaty to ban chemical weapons and the strengthening of the existing ban on biological weapons might be effective if assertive arrangements for disclosure and active monitoring are developed on an international scale. It is obvious, however, that prevailing controls on conventional weapons, particularly those affecting advanced conventional weapons, are not likely to succeed without fundamental redesign of the control system. That weakness threatens controls in the other weapons categories as well.

In the United States at the moment six separate arrangements control the international diffusion of nuclear weapons, chemical weapons, biological agents, ballistic missile technology, standard conventional munitions, and dual-use technology. In each case, there are substantial differences in the legislative basis for control, the administrative apparatus that executes control, the operational practices that have evolved over time, the arrangements for international collaboration, and the effectiveness achieved. There has been no systematic attempt to integrate these separate activities into a comprehensive control program. Such integration could strengthen all six regimes by unifying control bureaucracies and procedures for efficiency, sharing verification and transparency measures synergistically, and depoliticizing individual applications of the controls. As yet no attempt has been made to establish cooperation on an integrated control program among the major countries that supply most of the weapons and most of the relevant technology. No attempt has been made to establish principles of equity that might make an integrated control policy operating among the major suppliers acceptable to the international community as a whole. It is a reasonable presumption that without substantial integration, cooperation with and acceptance of each of the separate control arrangements will erode with time.

Clearly a redesigned weapons control arrangement entailing integration of existing control regimes, cooperation among the chief suppliers, and general international acceptance is a demanding enterprise, but again, there are some practical advantages to build on. In the aftermath of the Persian Gulf War, all of the states of that region, including the large oil exporters, are carrying large debt burdens and are disillusioned with the results of their previous arms purchases. The financial aftermath of the Gulf War and sluggish economic performance throughout the world have shrunk the international arms market so much that none of the major suppliers can expect to do very well through standard forms of competition, however assertive individual suppliers attempt to be. That circumstance, which is unique in the past forty years, provides a window of opportunity to cooperatively organize the much smaller market that is emerging and to manage the industrial restructuring that will inevitably be imposed.

For the weapons producers emerging from the old Warsaw Pact and the dissolved Soviet Union, this is a compelling matter. They are caught up in a large-scale organizational and economic conversion that precludes the continuation of their traditional practices. To survive they must secure access to capital and technology from international markets, and they must adjust their business practices and product lines to that requirement. For them radical redirection is a foregone conclusion. For their Western counterparts it is more of a question, but very few of them can confidently project the continuation of traditional patterns of business. The industrial structure that designs and produces weapons has strong reason to accept, even to seek, the comprehensive international regulation of weapons sales and related technology that a cooperative security arrangement would require. Counteracting this logic is the temptation of former Warsaw Pact nations to sell surplus weapons from inventory as a means of providing desperately needed hard currency to ease the pain of their economic restructuring programs. Western nations should be exploring the option of buying these surplus weapons (at minimal prices) and scrapping them. That may prove to be a lower-cost option than having to destroy them on the battlefield at some later time.

Transparency

A cooperative security system involving extensive agreed-on constraints on military preparations would have to require all parties to accept a level of intrusive monitoring of their defense programs. First, such transparency would apply to force size and equipment, as in the START and CFE agreements. It would extend to major exercises and selected military operations, as in the European CSBMs, certain super-power agreements covering accidents and potentially hazardous military activities, and the Camp David accords. Second, it would cover certain development, test, and manufacturing activities, as in START, the INF, the ABM treaty, the Nonproliferation treaty, and the biological and chemical weapons conventions. And third, it would apply to sales and purchases of military-related activities, as in START, the ABM treaty (forbidding transfer of weapons to other states), COCOM, the Perm Five agreement on conventional arms sales, and the nuclear, biological, and chemical weapons regimes. For the control of nuclear, biological, and chemical weapons especially, a cooperative regime permitting regular inspection, including challenge inspections, would strengthen all three sets of limits in a mutually reinforcing way.

Such an international regime of transparency would mean greater sharing of national intelligence, as well as cooperatively established "international technical means" of monitoring in the fields of, for example, missile warning, air traffic surveillance, satellite photography, and cooperatively emplaced ground sensors on national territory (for detecting movement of tanks, launch of missiles, underground nuclear detonations, and so on). These measures could be implemented by an International Assessment Agency, created by the United Nations, which would receive agreed-on data from national collection systems, as well as from its own collection systems (for example, the agency could be the international body responsible for operating an Open Skies collection system). These transparency measures must be accompanied by an international consensus of opinion that interprets concealment of suspect military facilities and activities as hostile intent, subject to the same penalties as outright violation.

Control strategies for exports, especially for dual-use technology and for certain aspects of nuclear, biological, and chemical weapons pro-liferation, are currently based on denial of access to advanced technology (as, for example, in COCOM). This emphasis should give way to a control strategy stressing much freer availability of technology to all states for peaceful economic growth if such states agree to free disclosure of sale, purchase, and use. States cooperating, provided they were open about intended end use, would enjoy relatively unencumbered access to the technology of the advanced industrial states, including to weapons systems consistent with the principle of defensive configuration.

In this regard, the radical advances in the processing and transmission of information that are a major factor driving the problem of weapons proliferation also offer some significant opportunities for devising responses. If disclosure is made the primary basis for regulation, then some very effective measures could be introduced to facilitate monitoring and enforcement without disrupting normal trade flows. An international registry could be established to record the manufacturer, the user, and the end use of all weapons products, major components, and sensitive technologies. Encoded labels could be attached to all these items supplying the information that had been sent to the registry. The labels could be designed so they could be updated according to changing circumstances and could not be successfully manipulated or detached without giving reliable evidence of that fact. (Direct labeling of chemical and biological agents would be technically more demanding but not inconceivable.)

If full disclosure were the norm, then unregistered products or products without labels would be illegal. Individuals involved with such products would be subject to criminal proceedings, and states in violation would be subject to international sanctions. Monitoring of the registry and selected inspection of products would make it much more difficult to conceal clandestine national weapons programs or international transfers. It would also provide the basis for bringing sanctions to bear. Access to trade credits and other sources of international capital could be made contingent, for example, on participation in the registry and compliance with its rules.

The requirements for reporting and product labeling would impose some regulatory burden, but that is not likely to deter cooperation. The chief weapons manufacturers have long been subject to requirements for documentation and approval of transfers, and a systematized registry would not be a large change. Western enterprises that manufacture and trade dual-use products have long adhered to cumbersome requirements for prior approval under arrangements set up by COCOM. These arrangements, which were directed against the old Soviet Union and its Warsaw treaty allies, have lost their original political rationale, but there will be strong inclination to continue them against newly identified targets such as Iraq. Instead of this increasingly futile apparatus based on prior approval, an international registry and regulating regime founded on disclosure would actually reduce the regulatory burden for most of the affected industry.

An international registry seems feasible. It would enforce disclosure of weapons manufacturers and transfers, embody agreed-on restrictions on weapons deployments, set requirements for arms sales and other types of transfers to be consistent with the ceilings, and monitor categorical prohibition of weapons of mass destruction. If the principal weapons suppliers—primarily the United States, United Kingdom, Germany, France, Russia, China, and Japan—used such a registry to coordinate their arms deployments, transfers, and technical trade, the core of an international cooperative security arrangement would thereby be formed, and powerful inducements could be offered to all countries to comply with the arrangement.

Countries participating in the cooperative security arrangement and complying with its rules would face lessened physical threat from other nations, would have access to extremely valuable security information, and ultimately to traditional collective security guarantees from all the other members. Countries not participating would be denied the information but, even more meaningfully, would stand in potential confrontation with the international community as a whole. Only countries in compliance with the arrangement would have access to the international lending institutions or to any form of publicly subsidized credit. With a systematic pattern of disclosure established and national intelligence assets using that base to monitor compliance, systematic violation would be a very great risk for defiant individuals, organizations, or states—much more of a risk than they have ever faced before. National governments trying to develop military power outside the cooperative regime would face real economic penalties, and military leaders and arms industries would have to contend with their own economic ministers and civil industries before subjecting the nation to the risk of becoming a pariah in the international arena.

Motivations for Security Cooperation

In broad outline at least, the idea of cooperative security has conceptual and practical coherence. It cannot be dismissed as infeasible. But feasibility is one thing and accomplishment is quite another. The basic notion of reliable security cooperation clearly labors against the pervasive emotions and institutionalized practices of national rivalry. If realization of the idea depended entirely on prevailing attitudes, the prospects would be remote indeed.

But immediate political opinion is not the entire story. In recent years, some very entrenched attitudes and political structures have suddenly crumbled, thereby revealing underlying forces powerful enough to revise the axioms of international politics. Eastern Europe and the Soviet Union have been caught up in a transformation that is unquestionably altering the character of these societies and resonating throughout the world. Although the details of cause and effect are still elusive, the impetus for this transformation has evidently emerged from the industrial democracies but is largely spontaneous in nature. The propagation of a market economy and the promotion of political democracy have long been rhetorical pieties among the Western nations, but there was no design for the process unleashed in Eastern Europe—no formulated intention or systematically pursued policy with a plausible claim to have been the conscious agent of these events. The industrial democracies are themselves caught up in the transformation and are discovering its implications on virtually the same schedule as everyone else.

At least some of the driving forces are obvious. A progressive internationalization of economic activity is breaking down ideologically imposed barriers and forcing conformity to a common set of operating rules. That is to say, an integrated international economy is forming. This development is largely spontaneous. Its logic and policy requirements have yet to be fully mastered, but almost certainly the problems of management it poses will transcend the capacity of any national government, however willful. Most likely, the emerging international economy will eventually compel far more sophisticated and more pervasive international coordination than nations have been accustomed to.

This development is being driven by a revolution in the processing and transmission of information. Over recent decades, the handling of information has undergone the most radical gains in raw capacity and efficiency in economic history, and the consequences of that progress are just beginning to unfold. Among other things, access to advanced technology is widening, and that reality is altering the technical circumstances in which defense investments are made.

Moreover, as information, technology, and economic activity diffuse, so do formative attitudes. Across wide differences in history and culture, an imperative to establish political authority more on the basis of social consensus than on coercion seems to be emerging. Compliance with this imperative is probably a necessary condition for operating an economy that performs at world standards. Conversely, economic performance is probably a necessary condition for viable political authority. This interaction appears to establish a powerful connection between national politics and international circumstance for virtually all countries of the world. However strong the impulse to project a separate national or ethnic identity and however pressing domestic priorities may be, it does not appear that international detachment can be achieved or that confrontation with world standards can be sustained. Some international collaboration has become a presumed requirement for operating an economy that prospers. Conversely, standing at odds with the international community through some transgression of its established norms can be made to have very serious economic consequences for pariah nations.

Looming somewhat more ambiguously but nonetheless detectably on the horizon is the matter of global environmental constraints. The population base of the world economy is currently in a stage of explosive exponential growth. More than 5 billion humans are currently seeking their livelihood, and that base will grow by a factor of 2 to 3 toward the end of the next century before stabilizing somewhere in the range of 9 to 14 billion—an uncertainty band equal to the current population. With modest progress made toward more evenly distributed standards of living and modest growth in the leading economies, the total world economy will grow by a factor of between 5 and 7 as the population surge reaches its crest.

The level of this projected world economy and the rate of growth are unprecedented. The consequences cannot yet be defined with the confidence necessary to define appropriate policies. Nonetheless one can prudently presume that major biophysical constraints will be encountered having to do with the composition of the atmosphere and with the cycling of basic nutrients and toxic chemicals. These matters are capable of giving the familiar phrase "vital interest" far more compelling meaning than it has had previously. Within a decade vital interests of this sort will probably begin to alter the international security agenda. Conceivably within four decades—the span of the cold war—such vital interests will absolutely dominate it. The consequences of such a development are difficult to determine at this point, but obviously there will be no substitute for effective international collaboration. If global economic constraints do appear, they will impose the logic of cooperation on even the most recalcitrant nationalists.

Large forces reshaping the patterns of history do not easily enter the idiom of immediate politics, however. Practical decisions made by some form of consensus are necessarily framed in familiar terms. The salience of the concept of cooperative security is suggested by these broad shaping patterns, but its adoption will be driven by immediate problems that are urgently on the security agenda and that set the larger underlying forces in a more familiar and comprehensible context. There are several issues that have this potential to compel attention to the attractions of the cooperative security concept. Skeptics about cooperative security have to contend with these powerful motivating problems.

The Danger of Uncontrolled Disintegration of the Former Soviet Union's Military Establishment

Whatever outcome the internal transformation of the old Soviet Union might ultimately produce, the military establishment the Soviet Union created will be profoundly altered. The successor states of the new Commonwealth are gripped by an extended economic crisis that is imposing large reductions on defense expenditures. They cannot sustain the forces they have inherited at anything like their size of recent decades. Those forces, and the defense industry that supplied them, will necessarily undergo a precipitous contraction. Moreover, the planning mechanisms needed to design a coherent outcome and to control the process of transition have been severely disrupted by the collapse of the central government. Reconstituting the capacity for managing the military establishment depends on settling fundamental constitutional and economic issues that cannot readily be made to march to the schedule required by force structure planning.

This situation has several stark implications for international security. Not only does it preclude any invasion of Western Europe, it reverses the physical basis for that conception of threat. Unless the major military powers in Europe and Asia reduce their forces in tandem, the states of the new Commonwealth will not be able to remain convinced of the safety of the path they are on, nor will the smaller members of the Commonwealth be able to do so with respect to neighboring Russia. Moreover, management of the process of demobilization is a prime internal security consideration. The integrity of political authority in these states bears more directly on their security than any traditional measure of external threat they might theoretically postulate. For the states of the Commonwealth and for the international community as well, responsible management of the large existing inventories of conventional and nuclear weapons is the most immediately compelling security issue. That fact dictates that all must cooperate in subordinating traditional military considerations to the interests of secure managerial control.

This new imperative of internal control has been recognized as it applies to nuclear weapons. The Nunn-Lugar legislation has initiated a process of engagement between the United States and the Commonwealth states for the purpose of consolidating control over nuclear weapons. That compelling focus has provided political impetus and a practical context for working out the details of cooperation. But this initial, narrowly defined objective cannot be achieved unless the process of cooperation is extended to conventional forces as well.

Despite the special organizational arrangements for handling nuclear weapons that developed in both the United States and the former Soviet Union, their operations have been sufficiently integrated into overall military activity so that an effective approach to consolidating control cannot exclude conventional forces. This condition is especially true for the ground forces that have been the larger part and the organizational core of the traditional Soviet establishment. They are most seriously affected by the impending demobilization, and their fate has a stronger effect on most of the issues endemic to internal security. It is extremely unlikely that secure control of nuclear weapons could be maintained while the Red Army disintegrates.

Neither the Commonwealth itself nor its constituent states can be expected to handle the necessary reconfiguration of their conventional military forces without substantial international collaboration. Without the cover of international restraints on conventional forces, they might not believe themselves able to match the legitimate requirements of territorial defense with their available forces, and they might be driven into primary reliance on nuclear weapons. Such a development would burden the integrated nuclear control that has been agreed on among the successor states but that cannot be taken for granted. The graceful apportionment of inherited conventional forces by members of the Commonwealth is an issue that could easily trigger internal conflict dangerous to economic and political reform.

Worldwide Restructuring of Military Establishments and Arms Markets

Linked to the looming contraction of the military establishment of the former Soviet Union is an enormous problem of social welfare. Millions of soldiers and their dependents will need housing and new jobs. Even more catastrophic in many ways is the plight of the military industry in the former Soviet Union, where the number of wage earners and their dependents threatened by the steep downturn in state orders for weapons systems figures in the tens of millions. Success in conversion of defense industries to civil production is essential, moreover, to success in overall economic reform and to political reform and stability. A restive technical and managerial elite in the previously privileged military-industrial complex poses the greatest threat to the new democratic spirit in the former Soviet Union—greater than any consumer revolt or backlash. Political leaders in these countries will be strengthened if they can claim that these painful restructurings are part of an international cooperative design, if they can point to active assistance from Western countries, and if they can point to analogous processes of difficult retrenchment in Western military industries.

Indeed, in Western nations too, massive demobilization is very contentious politically. The process is much less significant economically than it is in the former Soviet Union, since it affects a much smaller share of GNP and is taking place in large, flexible market economies. Nevertheless, demobilization has its political opponents even in Western countries. A natural place for threatened defense industries to look for new markets, moreover, is in the international arms trade. A cooperative security arrangement that relates these politically difficult defense restructurings to a larger international purpose and that exhibits the fact that all countries are sharing in the pain is essential for allowing the desired post–cold war contraction to take place and for preventing proliferation through increased arms exports.

Finally, in most countries caught in regional security dilemmas, there are analogous trade-offs between military investment and civil investment necessary for economic development. These trade-offs have political salience, as economic and military officials contend for the ear of national leaders. Here too, cooperative security would give international legitimacy to desirable trends toward demilitarization.

Operational Safety and Security of Nuclear Arsenals

As long as the threat of sudden attack was considered the primary security problem, the safe management of weapons was accepted as a subordinate, though important, consideration. Extensive provisions were developed to protect against the accidental or unauthorized explosion of any nuclear weapon as well as against any compromise of physical custody. These provisions were all designed, however, to preserve a large inventory of weapons in an extremely responsive state of deployment. The primary objective of deterrence required the continuously available ability to initiate a large nuclear weapons attack within a few minutes and to complete it in a few hours. The danger of a prior attack on the deterrent forces required that under emergency circumstances it be possible to disperse this capability to a relatively large number of widely separated weapons commanders. These commitments to rapid response, dispersed control, and large-scale attack programming made operational safety inherently more difficult to achieve.

The record of experience, as best it can be determined, has been extremely good despite the difficulty. No unintended nuclear detonations have occurred, and the only known compromises of physical custody have been the result of operational accidents whose frequency seems to have diminished with accumulating experience. Indefinite extrapolation of this experience is nonetheless a serious question. The internal pressures on the strategic command system of the former Soviet Union are so extensive and of such uncertain consequence that its ability to maintain standards of safety while preserving a highly reactive operational posture cannot prudently be assumed.

Moreover, the possibility that the two strategic forces could accidentally trigger each other because of their highly reactive postures is an enduring problem that simply cannot be measured on the basis of experience to date. The strategic nuclear forces have never been subjected to the intense pressures that their standard alert procedures would impose on each other under crisis conditions. In particular, the warning systems that mediate the critical judgment as to whether a nuclear attack is or is not in progress have never encountered the unique flows of information and problems of interpretation that a full process of alerting forces would create. It cannot be presumed that the probability of a catastrophic misjudgment would remain as low in crisis as it certainly has been under the peacetime and mild crisis circumstances encountered to date. The system has not yet been tested under severe stress.

The various initiatives that have been undertaken to reduce nuclear weapons deployments and to relax routine alert procedures will alleviate but not eliminate the internal pressures on the strategic command system of the Commonwealth. They will have very little material effect on the underlying problem of crisis interaction. The commitment to rapid reaction has not been altered, and traditional crisis alert procedures remain in effect on both sides, as does the pattern of dispersed control. Even the sharply reduced forces and reconfigured weapons deployments that are to result from the June 1992 framework agreement are capable of inflicting enormous damage on any industrial society. In fact, even at these lower force levels, an inadvertent triggering of the strategic attack plans that are being continued as the basis for deterrence would still be the largest man-made catastrophe in history. Given the inherent inability to determine the probability of such an event, there is strong reason to seek higher standards of safety by removing the commitment to rapid reaction and dispersed control.

Deterrence is now accepted as less urgent and easier to achieve. Thus, even without eliminating the confrontational deployments that give rise to the inherent dangers, greater scope now exists for improving operational safety. Standards of safety as exacting as those demanded of nuclear reactors would almost certainly require, however, that alert deployments be terminated; that is, all nuclear weapons must be held in a state that would require some visible and time-consuming preparation to be completed before they could be used. In order to ensure adequate protection in such a state of deployment, extensive cooperation in the design and maintenance of operational procedures would undoubtedly be needed. Since the power of the deterrent effect would hardly be affected by imposing, say, a week of preparations required to implement it, provided the preparation times applied to all nuclear weapon states, the greater operational safety provided by a nonalert posture is a strong incentive for cooperation.

Technological Diffusion and Proliferation

The memorable rise of a world economy driven by large-scale increases in the international flows of information have already profoundly altered the conditions for making technical investments in security.

Besides the five formally acknowledged nuclear weapons states, more than ten other countries have the immediate technical potential to deploy a significantly destructive nuclear weapons capability if they choose to do so. Approximately the same countries have plausible capacities to produce ballistic missiles or cruise missiles and have ready access to advanced sensing and information-processing technologies that are the chief ingredients of advanced conventional munitions. The traditional policies of controlling the diffusion of weapons of mass destruction, advanced delivery vehicles, and their necessary support services by denying access to materials and information have been decisively undermined by technical diffusion. National choice, not technical access, has become the decisive factor.

Most of the major industrial countries have made their choices about nuclear and chemical weapons. The number of states that maintain overtly deployed nuclear weapons has held at five for three decades. Several other major industrial states, such as Germany, Japan, Canada, and Italy, who could readily produce deployed forces in these categories have shown no inclination to do so. They continue to support the nonproliferation treaty and the impending chemical weapons convention that is designed to remove all existing stocks of chemical weapons. Four states—Israel, India, Pakistan, and South Africa—are usually assumed to have acquired nuclear weapons capabilities of minimal to modest size but so far have not engaged in actively displayed deployments. Their measured step beyond the threshold has been recognized for some years by most of the world. The diffusion of technology has strained but not yet destroyed the prevailing structure of control.

It is unlikely that this equilibrium will be sustained, however, without significantly strengthening and formalizing the arrangements for national restraint. An apparent nuclear weapons program in North Korea and a potential one in Iran are not under reliable control. Active nuclear weapons deployments by either or both of these countries would probably shatter the political accommodation that has evolved so far and might trigger nuclear weapons programs in inherently more capable countries that have so far desisted. Even if that reaction could be prevented, uncontrolled programs of this sort in radical states are very likely to stimulate assertive development of advanced conventional forces by their neighbors.

Advanced conventional weapons capability is based on the integrated combination of several basic functions: frequent wide-area surveillance;

rapid extraction of relevant information from ample surveillance data; rapid dissemination of this information and integration into operational plans; and extremely precise navigation to designated targets with vehicles that are difficult to detect. Once this combination of functions is fully mastered, a military organization could in principle identify and attack any visible target of a few square meters in size anywhere in the world in less than an hour. That produces a highly intrusive type of capability that has never before been available: extremely efficient violence with exact precision in time and place at indefinitely long range. Fully competitive development of this capability would enable an array of coercive actions that would pose security problems of an entirely new character. No head of state or politically controversial figure could travel or give a public speech in complete confidence. No fixed installation above ground would be secure from a surprise, and possibly devastating, attack.

Fortunately time and effort still offer meaningful protection from this situation. After fifteen years of intense investment, the United States alone has entered the initial stages of this type of capability, and even U.S. achievements so far remain short of full technical potential. Because it requires the integration of many functions and technical components, the development of an advanced reconnaissance strike capability cannot emerge as quickly as the underlying revolution in information handling that enables it. No other military organization is within a decade of matching the United States in this respect, and the United States is more than a decade away from complete realization of the development it has pioneered. The problem of regulating reconnaissance strike capability has nonetheless been inexorably posed. A security nightmare looms and its prevention creates a powerful incentive for cooperative arrangements.

The current lead the United States enjoys in reconnaissance strike capability creates a grave temptation to neglect the longer-term imperative and to rely on the immediate national comparative advantage conferred. There are some strong current incentives, however, to discipline this tendency. If there is no military organization in position to match the United States quickly, there are many in position to negate it, at least in local areas, by targeting critical assets. Aircraft carriers, Airborne Warning and Control System (AWACS) aircraft and satellites, for example, are, on the one hand, critical ingredients of the U.S. capability and, on the other hand, exceedingly vulnerable to a limited form of such a capability in the hands of an opponent. A lesser power can aspire to attack the information sensors in our reconnaissance strike complex much more readily than to create full-fledged counterparts. Moreover, many countries that feel threatened by an intrusive reconnaissance strike capability they cannot match can aspire to chemical agents as a strategic counterweight. The United States is highly exposed to chemical destructive agents delivered by small aircraft or clandestine means. Despite its advantages in nuclear and conventional weapons operations, therefore, the United States faces problems of weapons proliferation strong enough to motivate fundamental changes in its own security thinking.

Biotechnology and Biological Warfare

Despite the close comparison to chemical agents that is frequently assumed, biotechnology presents, in fact, a unique threat and a fundamentally different problem of control. The distinction begins with the obvious and important fact that biological agents can regenerate themselves and spread from one person to another. That simple feature creates the theoretical possibility of tremendously destructive consequences. An agent that could defeat the human immune system and spread efficiently could threaten a significant portion of the entire world population.

Fortunately in the long process of evolution, human defenses have dominated the various offensive strategies of the organisms that attack them, and so far that balance has been quite robust. Though many tens of biological agents have been identified that are capable of producing life-threatening infections in humans hosts, they all reflect a basic trade-off that has enabled human survival. The most rapid and efficient killers—anthrax, for example, that was prominently feared during the Persian Gulf War—spread so inefficiently that they give ample time for natural or organized containment. The most efficient spreaders—influenza, for example—generally do not have lethal effects. Mutant agents produced by genetic engineering techniques have so far tended to be less vigorous in their effects than naturally evolved organisms and to be subject to the same trade-off between lethality and efficiency of propagation.

There is no reason to believe, however, that this trade-off is an immutable law of nature, and there is every reason to believe that rapidly progressing understanding of the genetic code will deliver tremendous power over biological interactions. That power will almost certainly confer the ability to produce major, indeed massive, consequences for good and for ill. Power of that magnitude will compel commensurately effective management.

This prospect has already descended from the level of informed speculation to immediate practical significance. In recent years, techniques for manipulating the influenza virus have been identified. Influenza has the most effective mechanism of transmission of all known biological organisms. Some strains have demonstrated the ability to infect 80 percent of the total human world population within a six-month period. Influenza can also be highly lethal. Some strains, which happen to infect birds rather than humans, have killed virtually all of the infected population. The immune resistance to influenza infection embodied in the current world population is sensitive to differences in strain type—that is, to the range of mutations that regularly occur. These facts suggest that a highly efficient and highly lethal influenza could be deliberately created; indeed, such a strain could emerge naturally. The world at the moment is very poorly organized for prevention or for effective reaction. Cooperation is an essential element of managing biotechnology for this or for any other purpose.

Because neither known nor projected biological agents are competitive with explosives or with chemical agents in tactical military applications, their development has not been a central commitment of military organizations. Even the most virulent biological agents require too much time to work their lethal effects to be of use in immediate battles, and the major military establishments have focused on immediate battles rather than on wanton strategic destruction. Moreover, any temptations to biological warfare have been checked by the obvious danger of falling victim to one's own actions.

The Biological Weapons Convention of 1972 prohibits the development, production, storage, or use of biological agents as weapons but allows research for defense or prophylactic purposes. Since the distinction between legitimate and prohibited activities was not specified beyond those general formulations, there has been legal ambiguity and intense suspicion about research activities on biological agents conducted by military organizations. That suspicion has been strengthened following the dissolution of the Soviet Union by allegations from Russian sources that preparations were made during the Soviet period for the production of biological agents on a scale that would unambiguously contradict the 1972 convention.

However, the development of biotechnology has been primarily conducted not by military organizations but by national medical establishments whose basic purposes are legitimate and compelling. Virtually all the relevant information and materials have necessarily been made widely accessible. There is no prospect whatsoever of denying access in the manner that has been used to protect nuclear materials and weapons design information.

Managerial control of the dangers and opportunities of biotechnology must rest on complete transparency of relevant activity and active international monitoring. These imperatives will eventually be powerful enough to overwhelm embedded resistance. The practical question is whether international cooperation will be accepted on the basis of reasonable prediction or whether some disastrous experience will be necessary to make the point.

Competing Needs for Technological Investment

A lessened pace of investment in military forces should be reflected in a lesser dedication of scientific and technological resources to weapons research and development. Indeed, the opportunity to address other human needs is itself an important motivation in the quest to achieve cooperative limits on military spending. The significance of such a diversion varies among the Western nations, the countries of the former Eastern bloc, and the developing world. But everywhere technology is recognized as critical to the economic performance of industry. All nations could benefit from new energy, transportation, and telecommunications infrastructures, suitably adapted to local circumstances.

The growing scale of human activity, combined with the increasing knowledge of the relationship between human activity and the prospects for sustainable development, create a demand for environmental monitoring and management technologies that can be expected to grow explosively in coming decades. And militarily, emphasis must shift from developing new weapons to enhancing the safety and security of existing forces, dismantling the nuclear and chemical weapons surplus of the cold war and cleaning up production facilities and bases, and developing the technologies of cooperative monitoring and verification.

The significance of a technological peace dividend will probably be least pronounced in the United States, but still meaningful. Defense research and development still constitutes almost two-thirds of the federal government's annual research and development (R&D) spending, or—since government and private industry spend approximately equal amounts—almost one-third of total annual R&D spending in the United States. Thus the defense contribution to the overall national technology base is substantial. Redirection of a part of this defense-related spending to other purposes—whether public missions like health and the environment, or the economic advantage of the nation's private industry—could in principle produce markedly improved results. But there are reasons to discount the technological peace dividend in the United States and other Western industrialized nations, at least in comparison to the former Eastern bloc and the less developed countries of the rest of the world

For one thing, the large cuts looming for the U.S. defense budget will not be matched by proportionately large reductions in defense R&D spending. The Pentagon's expressed intention is to continue to spend heavily on technology so that the U.S. military, while smaller, will sustain its qualitative edge over that of any other nation. Whether the results of the highly political defense budget process will correspond to this expressed intention is, of course, uncertain.

A much firmer reason to discount the overall significance of the technological peace dividend in the United States is the shrinking scale of defense R&D spending in relation to the overall technology base on which both public missions and private industry depend. This technology base consists of the national technology bases of all the countries with which the United States maintains rich and open contacts, that is, in practical terms, the aggregate of the technology bases of the countries of the Organization for Economic Cooperation and Development (OECD).

In the context of this aggregated technology base of the Western industrialized world, the significance of the U.S. Defense Department's contribution exhibits a striking decline over the past few decades. In 1960, fully one-third of all the R&D spending in the OECD countries, by governments and private companies combined, came from the Pentagon. By 1991, the Pentagon's fraction had fallen to 13 percent. The reason for this secular decline in the weight of the U.S. defense contribution to the world's leading-edge science and technology is simple: the Pentagon's technology spending increased by half in real terms between 1960 and 1991, but U.S. private industry increased R&D spending fourfold, and Japan, Germany, and the other OECD countries together increased their spending almost fivefold. This trend shows no sign of abating. Unless enormous *increases* take place in U.S. defense R&D spending, the Pentagon is fated to become a smaller and smaller force in shaping the technology base from which the leading industrial nations draw.

Consequently, the dividend to become available by reducing Pentagon R&D spending is losing significance as well. Furthermore, a reduction in the innovative effort of the Department of Defense does not automatically result in greater innovative effort elsewhere in the federal budget or in industry. Congress will not transfer each dollar of reduced Pentagon R&D to the budget of the National Institutes for Standards and Technology, the National Science Foundation, or the research arm of the Environmental Protection Agency. Nor will U.S. industry automatically employ defense scientists who are laid off.

Some transfer of defense talent to other purposes can be expected through the workings of the labor market for scientists and engineers. A glut of released defense talent bids down the wages of nondefense talent and thus results in more nondefense hiring of scientists and engineers. But labor markets for scientists and engineers are highly specialized and rarely conform to simple economic rules. Thus defense reductions by themselves, without a policy to redirect technological investment to civil purposes, might only result in less R&D being conducted. Though a civilian technology policy could be devised, so far little political conviction to do so has been manifested.

In the former Soviet Union, by contrast, the reduction of effort in defense technology at the end of the cold war can be expected to have a much more significant effect on the economy as a whole. The defense sector made up a much larger share of the economy of the former Soviet Union than of any Western nation—perhaps as much as 40 percent, in contrast to about 5 percent in the United States. The Soviet military has laid first claim to scientific talent and the best facilities for half a century. When a full accounting for both quantity and quality of the defense effort is measured, the share of the Soviet *technology* effort devoted to defense has perhaps been even larger than 40 percent. Thus the technology base of the former Soviet Union is an important potential contributor to economic development, to public infrastructure, and to the task of dismantling weapons and cleaning up military facilities. Recognition of this fact is widespread. However inefficient the current policy of "conversion" might be, it cannot fail to significantly affect the civil technology sector, which is woefully underdeveloped.

In other regions of the world, from Iraq and India to Brazil and Egypt, defense technology spending is similarly a drain on resources that could be devoted to economic development. Many emerging suppliers of weapons for the export trade outside of the major industrialized nations are also finding their fledgling defense industries in dire straits as the worldwide market for arms contracts. These nations face their own conversion processes. Moreover, governments are increasingly being held accountable for their nation's economic performance, directly where democracy has taken root but indirectly even where dictatorship prevails. And in many of these countries the sophistication of economic policymaking is increasing rapidly. There is therefore a cadre of economic development officials who can challenge the military for a share of the nation's technology investment and champion its redirection to civilian purposes before the national leadership. These officials receive tacit support for their case when international security cooperation suggests that defense spending can safely be reduced.

Substate and Civil Violence

The four decades of confrontation between two major alliances succeeded in preventing aggression of the variety that engulfed the world twice during the previous four decades. It did not succeed in preventing violence, however. Some 22 million people died in conflicts that were categorized as civil wars and internal insurgencies during the forty years of armed peace. A principle for guiding organized international approaches to this type of violence is badly needed. The principle of cooperative security applies mainly to the organized preparations of organized national military establishments and not to civil violence. But cooperative security contributes to, and indeed may be indispensable to, the development of an appropriate principle for organizing international approaches to substate violence.

Many substate conflicts have reflected the politics of alliance confrontation in Europe and were fueled by the supply of arms that emanated from it. Many conflicts have also moved dramatically toward political resolution as the global confrontation has dissolved—most notably, those in Cambodia, Afghanistan, Angola, Namibia, Nicaragua, and El Salvador. International political accommodation has clearly not removed the indigenous causes of violence, however, and in some cases it seems to have removed important restraints. As authoritarian political structures have crumbled under circumstances of severe economic austerity and as ethnic assertion and religious fundamentalism have surged into the vacuum created, spontaneous civil violence has emerged as an endemic problem in many parts of the world. Yugoslavia and Somalia are particularly destructive examples, but similar potential clearly exists in many other areas, perhaps most ominously in the successor states of the former Soviet Union.

As the bloodshed in Yugoslavia and Somalia reveals, the international community does not have the security mechanisms that would be required to control serious civil violence. The available apparatus of diplomatic mediation backed by the imposition of economic sanctions or even by threatened military intervention requires a corresponding political structure to have any constructive effect. But it is precisely the disintegration of internal political structures that lies at the core of the problem. It does no good to persuade or to coerce leaders who cannot implement decisions. If civil order has broken down to the extent that it cannot be internally reconstituted, then the only choices are to tolerate violence until it produces some self-limiting outcome or to intervene with sufficient strength to impose civil order. To date, tolerance has been the dominant choice by default. Intervention has been excluded as a practical matter, not for want of raw capability but rather because no country has been willing or able to construct the necessary consensus to intervene.

In light of emerging international circumstances no national government can or should assume the primary responsibility for imposing basic civil order when it has broken down in another sovereign entity. The implications of attempted hegemony and the risks of stimulating decisive international opposition because of those implications will dominate any calculus of national interest. This judgment is particularly true for the United States whose relative advantage in the military capacity for intervention creates proportionate international and domestic sensitivity. The continuation of tolerance by default could become exceedingly costly, however. The combination of economic austerity, ethnic conflict, and political disintegration is now so widespread that civil violence could become a general conflagration if tolerance remains the only realistic international option.

Since the control of civil violence is more a matter of national than of international interest, refined collaboration is almost certainly a necessary condition for dealing with it. For any intervention of the size and character necessary to impose civil order, it is prudent to assume that the costs, political risks, and operational burdens will have to be shared. A cooperative security arrangement systematically focused on preventing major aggression would not directly provide a standing force for this type of action but would certainly provide the context for creating such a force when it was required. The threat of widespread civil violence therefore gives significant indirect incentive to create the arrangement.

Some First Steps

If the period of the cold war can be summarized as a competition in military development, the emerging new era can be projected as a search for reliable control over the results of that competition. The primary security objectives of the major military establishment—deterrence and territorial defense—are not seriously in question, and their unresolved problems have to do with the secondary consequences of large existing deployments and advanced technical development. The reconfiguration of the Soviet military establishment, the interaction of strategic forces, the inexorable diffusion of weapons technology, the transcendent challenge of biotechnology, and the threat of widespread civil violence are all, in essence, problems of control. These problems might be solved in concert; they would assuredly be worsened by unregulated competition.

The imperatives of control are even more imposing for those countries that do not maintain large military establishments and do not have the resource base to develop them. Their perspective, however, is meaningfully different. Countries without powerful military establishments, particularly ones that are located within striking distance of countries that do have them, are unavoidably dependent on some form of international cooperation for their primary security objectives, as well as for their derivative ones. This fact raises the stakes they have in the process of cooperation but also tends to reduce the leverage they bring to bear. The political psychology of that situation is inevitably an important influence in forming a new international security arrangement.

The solution, if there is to be one, is not difficult to anticipate. A cooperative arrangement sufficiently well institutionalized to manage the driving problems of security means participants must respect the sovereignty of one another. The major military establishments will have to contain their military investments and subordinate the projection of their power to matters of international interest rather than national prerogative. Moreover, they will have to establish reasonable equity, in substance and procedure, in determining what international interest means. For their part states with lesser military establishments will have to align their aspirations with standards of equity that can command international consensus and that exclude nationalist or divisive ideological assertions. They will have to relinquish the obstructionist policies and clandestine conspiracies that have frequently been used to seek some marginal shift in national advantage against the inherently stronger states.

But an outcome of this sort develops in stages rather than by a sudden act of creation, no matter how powerful the forces that drive change. Instruments of control, institutionalization of cooperation, and corresponding rules of equity will undoubtedly evolve in partial measures and thin layers. In practical terms, the first of these steps have more immediate significance than the last. In fact, some of the first steps have already been taken and have produced enough experience to build on for the future.

Superpower Denuclearization

The developing engagement between the United States and the Commonwealth states in dismantling nuclear weapons and redirecting weapons designers is one of the important immediate steps for which the intention to cooperate has been authoritatively formulated. Some effort has also been made to work out the implications of this decision. The results of this cooperative effort will determine the scope and character of subsequent development. Initially, this effort included an offer for unilateral extensions of U.S. financial and technical assistance for the process of warhead decommissioning and redirection of weapons design personnel occurring in the Commonwealth. This offer was made in advance of any specific determination of Commonwealth needs and without any offer of reciprocal involvement in the corresponding processes in the United States. Since enduring cooperation undoubtedly requires more balance in the relationship and, eventually, more inclusive international participation as well, working out appropriate reciprocity between the United States and the Commonwealth and extending the arrangements to the other nuclear weapons states is an obvious area for development.

Ground Force Relocation

It seems both likely and desirable that a second pattern of engagement will develop to deal with the disposition of conventional ground forces. The process of implementing the CFE treaty will require some international understanding of the distributions of treaty-limited equipment among the Commonwealth states. Additional international assistance will probably be required to complete the process of removing the forces of the former Soviet Union from their positions in Eastern Europe. Some 195,000 former Soviet military officers are currently without housing even though the entire military construction budget is being devoted to that purpose. Germany is providing 36,000 housing units under the unification agreement—half of which are planned for construction in the Ukraine, reflecting the anticipated distribution of forces when the Soviet Union remained intact. It would be a reasonable extension of this arrangement for the international community to expand assistance in the construction of housing for military officers and to distribute the construction in accord with the eventual distribution of forces among the Commonwealth states. This would be an appropriately focused and unusually effective expression of cooperative intent.

Greater Military-to-Military Contacts and Planning Dialogue

A broader and more venturesome extension of this element of engagement would mean explicit discussion of end-state force size, defense budget levels, and doctrinal justification among the major establishments. For the Russian Federation and other Commonwealth states, active deployments are virtually certain to fall well below CFE ceilings, and in their new political process defense budgets will be discussed more candidly in public. The mission aspirations of the reduced establishment will probably still be considered a very sensitive topic but are unlikely to include anything that could not in principle be productively discussed with the Western military establishments.

Among the Western military establishments, fiscal pressures and competing economic priorities are also very likely to drive force deployments below the levels embodied in the CFE ceilings. In the leading instance, U.S. military planners are currently projecting $1.7 trillion in outlays over the next six years to support a force structure reduced some 25 percent below 1990 levels. The planners are attempting to justify that effort in terms of traditional preparedness against a now unspecified set of potential enemies. In the absence of plausible scenarios in which U.S. forces might be required in large numbers on short notice, it seems unlikely that the dollar amount or the standard planning axioms will survive competition with domestic priorities.

Military planners whose careers were formed during the cold war will not readily adopt doctrines of inclusive security cooperation as a philosophical conviction, but they do much better in the actual practice of it. During the Gorbachev years enough contact developed between Soviet military officers and their Western counterparts to demonstrate that both sides are personally and professionally responsive to appropriate collaboration. Much of the content of this military dialogue has been symbolic and rhetorical, but it could readily be given more meaningful content. If the respective military planners were authorized to brief one another on their force structure targets, budget projections, and underlying doctrinal assumptions, they would almost certainly develop a sense of mutual interest.

Under the budget reductions that perspective will be imposed for overriding economic reasons. The major establishments can achieve better security with higher-quality forces at lower levels of deployment if they collaborate. If they were also authorized to experiment with joint operations, the respective military establishments would quickly learn how to manage collaborative security policies on that level as well.

Common Warning and Intelligence Functions

In the early phases of developing a cooperative arrangement, the joint conduct of military missions would probably be limited to occasional experimental exercises, but for a few important support functions sustained cooperation is already a serious prospect. Official proposals have been made for collaboration in tactical warning of missile launches, a most promising and important area for development. The underlying problem of strategic force interactions is significantly affected by warning system performance and in fact depends heavily on a warning system function that is never tested, namely, a capacity to prove with high confidence that a strategic attack is not under way when there is heightened suspicion and some evidence that it might be. The warning system inherited by the CIS seems particularly vulnerable to that situation, and the loss of significant assets in the Baltic states will not help. If direct cooperation is allowed, many technical and operational innovations can alleviate this problem with few if any offsetting risks.

A more venturesome extension of common functions would be the common management of civil and military air traffic in all of Europe west of the Urals. Since tactical air operations depend on air traffic management and have emerged as the leading edge of any military operation, common management of air traffic is a powerful means of extending reassurance. The system would have to be terminated and replaced before any aggressive military operation could be undertaken.

Under the old alliance confrontation, Soviet and U.S. military air traffic was jointly managed in their respective areas by NATO and the WTO, and through their elaborate interactions, the two systems developed a great deal of familiarity with each other. The formal rivalry of the past could be transformed into direct collaboration, and the resulting internationalization of the system could readily become a principal element of cooperative security.

Arms Registration

The idea of establishing an international arms registry is probably the most important initial element in a consolidated management for controlling weapons proliferation. It has already achieved some formal standing and has inspired some unusual, if still rudimentary, diplomacy. In December 1991, twenty-six years after it first addressed the subject, the U.N. General Assembly passed a resolution calling for a voluntary registration of all arms exports and imports. One hundred fifty countries approved the resolution with no dissenting votes and only Cuba and Iraq abstaining. The only major defection was China, which, without explanation, did not participate in the vote. The strength of the vote ensures that some compliance will be achieved, and that prospect is being enhanced by informal discussions that do include China.

Beginning also in 1991, the permanent members of the U.N. Security Council began independent consultation outside of formal U.N. auspices to discuss the problem of arms transfers and the proliferation of weapons of mass destruction. In a series of meetings the U.N. participants discussed voluntary guidelines for regulating all arms transfers as well as special arrangements for notification and consultation with one another about arms transfers into the Middle East region. These discussions have not been given political priority by the participating governments and have not produced completed arrangements. They do reflect the beginning of consciousness and provide an established base for more serious development of the idea of an international registry.

Combining Proliferation Control Regimes

As noted, six distinct control regimes exist to cover nuclear, chemical, and biological weapons, missiles, conventional weapons, and dual-use items. The six regimes have had varied histories and political fortunes, and consequently different mechanisms of surveillance, control, and administration. The roles of participating member states have also varied. In the nations whose technology has been most important to control, nonproliferation has had low priority in comparison with the principal security task of waging cold war. As a result each of the control regimes took its opportunities for advancement when and where it could find them, and each one tried to steer clear of the political difficulties of the others.

If rhetoric about giving new priority to nonproliferation is to be translated into a concrete attempt to develop a truly comprehensive and global cooperative security regime, the question of how to structure these regimes for their common benefit is a logical one. The different regimes pose similar legal, regulatory, and administrative issues. They occasion similar political pressures from domestic firms intent on export. Violations experienced by all six regimes often involve the same arms traders and conduits of clandestine funding and thus pose common intelligence challenges.

In many countries nuclear, chemical, and biological weapons and missiles and other advanced conventional weapons are viewed by leaders as ways of garnering prestige and intimidating opponents. Their pursuit of all types of weapons is controlled by the same military or intelligence organs. The same security dilemmas animate efforts to acquire weapons of mass destruction. Stronger relationships among the currently rather weak international secretariats who administer international control regimes could result in intelligence sharing, common procedures for monitoring and inspections, preparation of lists of controlled items, and a combined effort to marshall political pressure behind cooperative control efforts.

Regional Cooperative Security Arrangements

Security cooperation has already been well developed in Europe. The entire history of the Conference on Security and Cooperation in Europe (CSCE) reflects the evolution of the basic idea, and the Paris Charter provides an authoritative statement of its basic principles. The Treaty on Conventional Armed Forces in Europe (CFE) imposes ceilings on major weapons categories for all members of the two historical alliance systems, and the Stockholm Agreement on Confidence and Security Building Measures provides rules for military force operations in the European area. Though these agreements were formulated in the context of the alliance confrontation that has now dissolved, their basic rules, especially their provisions for the exchange of information and direct monitoring of weapons and military activities, can readily be adapted to the new situation. The European states have practiced cooperation and have articulated political commitment to the idea well in advance of clearly establishing cooperative security as the central principle of their defense policies. This experience and the fact that Europe has been the primary focus of major power military engagement, offer a base and a model for practical evolution of the entire concept.

There are several major options for developing cooperative arrangements beyond the base that has been established in Europe. The first and most obvious one is to complete the European arrangements, especially the determination of the relationship between NATO and the former members of the Warsaw Pact. As a partial step into a new era, the North Atlantic Cooperation Council has been formed to plan regular consultations between the two groups of states, an innovation that acknowledges the dissolution of confrontation but also shows that residual suspicion has not been entirely overcome. The council is a device for giving the Eastern European and Commonwealth states observer status in NATO but not full membership. Full membership and the necessary redefinition of NATO are clearly the next steps to consider. In its complete form, these moves would include all CSCE members, thereby giving the CSCE the institutional apparatus it has never had.

Extending the European arrangements to other regions is essentially an open question at the moment. Since both the Russian Federation and the United States are powers in Asia as well as in Europe, it is not possible to develop completely systematic security arrangements for

Europe without including Asia. It would be possible to extend the CFE to Asia by a suitable adjustment of its terms, and that is an important option to consider. Conceivably an Asian equivalent of the CSCE might be attempted, although there is virtually no precedent, and so far the Asian states have shown little political inclination toward that idea.

The integration of East Asia by whatever method in the cooperative arrangements that have developed in Europe is clearly a necessary condition for forming a general international order, and in a minimal sense that may be a sufficient condition as well. The combination of Europe and East Asia would include the largest military establishments and the largest industrial economies. It could not be considered stable or complete, however, unless its rules and procedures were accepted in South Asia and in the Middle East. These extensions are clearly more difficult and presumably would have to come as subsequent developments. In completing the European security design, however, and in extending it to Asia, a strong consciousness of the requirements of global extension must be built into the design of any regional understanding.

* * *

In all these matters—the dismantling of warheads, the handling of existing treaty requirements, the initiation of new forms of dialogue, and the pursuit of regional institutions—existing states are evolving, in practical ways, a new security order in response to imperatives they do not fully understand but certainly do perceive in partial form. The idea of a cooperative security arrangement has not yet been conceptualized fully, accepted emotionally, or implemented systematically, but it has nonetheless manifested itself in various, concrete ways. Much of its future is yet to be determined, and the constructive outcome that can reasonably be envisaged is not guaranteed. Cooperative security will unavoidably be an important focus of political debate, however. Strong imperatives drive the new era of global cooperation, and their logic will command attention.